CONTRACT IN ROMAN LAW.

T0384575

THE ORIGIN AND HISTORY

OF

CONTRACT IN ROMAN LAW

DOWN TO

THE END OF THE REPUBLICAN PERIOD.

(BEING THE YORKE PRIZE ESSAY FOR THE YEAR 1893)

BY

W. H. BUCKLER, *B.A., LL.B.*

OF TRINITY COLLEGE, CAMBRIDGE.

LONDON:

C. J. CLAY AND SONS,

CAMBRIDGE UNIVERSITY PRESS WAREHOUSE,

AVE MARIA LANE.

1895

CAMBRIDGE
UNIVERSITY PRESS

University Printing House, Cambridge CB2 8BS, United Kingdom

Cambridge University Press is part of the University of Cambridge.

It furthers the University's mission by disseminating knowledge in the pursuit of education, learning and research at the highest international levels of excellence.

www.cambridge.org
Information on this title: www.cambridge.org/9781316623152

© Cambridge University Press 1895

First published 1895
First paperback edition 2016

A catalogue record for this publication is available from the British Library

ISBN 978-1-316-62315-2 Paperback

PREFACE.

IN treating so vast a subject within the narrow limits of an essay it is impossible to give a full description of every contract: I shall therefore assume the reader to be familiar with the ordinary terms and rules of Roman Law. It is equally impossible to discuss every debatable point on which historians have differed. Such works as the two large volumes by Bechmann on the history of Sale are indeed a rebuke to superficial scholarship; but the present essay professes only to be a sketch, and I shall be satisfied if I succeed in making the outlines clear.

W. H. B.

The following authorities have been consulted for the purposes of this essay:

Bachofen.	Das Pfandrecht.
Baron, I.	Geschichte des römischen Rechts. 1884.
	III Abhandl. aus dem röm. Civilpr. 1881.
Bechmann, C. G. A.	Der Kauf. 1876.
	Das röm. Dotalrecht.
Bekker, E. I.	Aktionen des röm. Privatrechts. 1871.
Bethmann-Hollweg.	Civilprozess.
Bruns, C. G.	Fontes iuris rom. antiqui. (5th Ed.)
Carnazza, G.	Il diritto commerciale dei Romani. 1891.
Christiansen.	Institutionen des röm. Rechts.
Clark, E. C.	Early Roman Law. 1872.
Costa, E.	Il dir. privato nelle commedie di Plauto.
	Le azioni exercitoria ed institoria.
Danz, H. A. A.	Lehrbuch der Gesch. des röm. Rechts. (2d Ed.) 1871.
	Der sacrale Schutz im röm. Rechtsverkehr. 1857.
Dernburg.	Das Pfandrecht.
Girtanner.	Die Stipulation. 1859.
	Ueber die Sponsio.
Gneist.	Die formellen Verträge. 1845.
Heimbach, G. E.	Lehre von dem Creditum. 1849.
Hugo.	Röm. Rechtsgeschichte.
Hunter.	Systematic Code of Roman Law. 1876.
Huschke.	Das Nexum. 1846.
Ihering, R. von	Geist des röm. Rechts. 1852.
Karlowa, O.	Civilprozess zur Zeit der L. Aktionen.
Karsten.	Die Stipulation. 1878.
Keller, F. L. von	Der röm. Civilprozess. (5th Ed.) 1876.
Leist.	Greco-Italische Rechtsgeschichte.
	Altarisches Ius Ciuile.
	Altarisches Ius Gentium.
	Geschichte der röm. Societas. 1881.
Lenel, O.	Das Edictum perpetuum. 1883.
Liebe.	Die Stipulation. 1840.

Meykow, R. von	Diction der röm. Brautgabe. 1850.
Maine, Sir H. S.	Ancient Law.
	Early History of Institutions.
Mommsen.	History of Rome (Dickson tr.). 1862.
	Gesch. des röm. Münzwesens. 1860.
	Stadtrechte von Salpensa, &c.
Moyle.	Institutes of Justinian.
Muirhead, J.	Private Law of Rome. 1886.
Muther.	Die Sequestration.
Ortolan.	Hist. of Roman Law (Eng. translation).
	1871.
Pernice, L. A. F.	M. Antistius Labeo. 1873.
Poste.	Gaius.
Pott, A. F.	Etymologische Forschungen. 1859.
Puchta.	Institutionen.
Rivier.	Untersuchungen ueber die Cautio, &c.
Rudorff, A. A. F.	Röm. Rechtsgeschichte. 1858.
	Das Edictum perpetuum. 1869.
Salpius.	Novation u. Delegation.
Savigny, F. C. von	Vermischte Schriften.
Schilling.	Institutionen.
Schlesinger.	Lehre von den Formalcontracten. 1858.
Ubbelohde.	Gesch. der benannten Realcontracten.
Voigt, M.	Röm. Rechtsgeschichte. Vol. 1. 1892.
	Die XII Tafeln. 1883.
	Lehre vom Ius Naturale. 1856—1876.
Walter.	Röm. Rechtsgeschichte.
Wunderlich, A.	De antiqua litterarum obligatione. 1832.

PERIODICALS.

Krit. Vierteljahrsschrift für gesch. Rechtswissenschaft.
Zeitschrift für Rechtsgeschichte.
Zeitschrift für Civilrecht und Prozess.
Nouvelle Revue historique de Droit.
Phil. Hist. Abhandlungen der kön. sächs. Gesellschaft der Wissenschaft.
Phil. Hist. Berichte (of the same).
Zeitschrift der Savigny Stiftung.   (Röm. Abtheilung.)

CONTENTS.

CHAPTER III.

CHAPTER IV.

CHAPTER V.

CHAPTER VI.

CHAPTER VII.

CHAPTER VIII.

INTRODUCTION.

WHOEVER has glanced through the pages of any text-book on Mercantile Law will hardly deny that Contract is the handmaid if not actually the child of Trade. Merchants and bankers must have what soldiers and farmers seldom need, the means of making and enforcing various agreements with ease and certainty. Thus, turning to the special case before us, we should expect to find that when Rome was in her infancy and when her free inhabitants busied themselves chiefly with tillage and with petty warfare, their rules of sale, loan, suretyship, were few and clumsy. Villages do not contain lawyers, and even in towns hucksters do not employ them. Poverty of Contract was in fact a striking feature of the early Roman Law, and can be readily understood in the light of the rule just stated. The explanation given by Sir Henry Maine is doubtless true, but does not seem altogether adequate. He points out[1] that the Roman household consisted of many families under the rule of a

---

[1] *Ancient Law*, p. 312.

paternal autocrat, so that few freemen had what we should call legal capacity, and consequently there arose few occasions for Contract. This may indeed account for the non-existence of Agency, but not for that of all other contractual forms. For if the households had been trading instead of farming corporations, they must necessarily have been more richly provided in this respect. The fact that their commerce was trivial, if it existed at all, alone accounts completely for the insignificance of Contract in their early Law.

The origin of Contract as a feature of social life was therefore simultaneous with the birth of Trade and requires no further explanation. It is with the origin and history of its individual forms that the following pages have to deal. As Roman civilization progresses we find Commerce extending and Contract growing steadily to be more complex and more flexible. Before the end of the Roman Republic the rudimentary modes of agreement which sufficed for the requirements of a semi-barbarous people have been almost wholly transformed into the elaborate system of Contract preserved for us in the fragments of the Antonine jurists.

CHAPTER I.

AT the most remote period concerning which statements of reasonable accuracy can be made, and which for convenience we may call the Regal Period, we can distinguish three ways of securing the fulfilment of a promise. The promise could be enforced either (1) by the person interested, or (2) by the gods, or (3) by the community. When however we speak of enforcement, we must not think of what is now called specific performance, a conception unknown to primitive Law. The only kind of enforcement then possible was to make punishment the alternative of performance.

I. Self-help, the most obvious method of redress in a society just emerging from barbarism, was doubtless the most ancient protection to promises, since we find it to have been not only the mode by which the anger of the individual was expressed, but also one of the authorised means employed by the gods or the community to signify their displeasure. This rough form of justice fell within the domain of Law in the sense that the law allowed it, and even encouraged men to punish the delinquent, whenever religion or custom had been violated. But as people grew more civilized and the nation larger, self-help must have proved a difficult and therefore inadequate remedy. Accordingly its scope was by degrees narrowed, and at last with the introduction of surer methods it became wholly obsolete.

II. Religious Law, as administered by the priests, the representatives of the gods, was another powerful agency for the support of promises. A violation of *Fides*, the sacred bond formed between the parties to an agreement, was an act of impiety which laid a burden on the conscience of the delinquent and may even have entailed religious disabilities. *Fides* was of the essence of every compact, but there were certain cases in which its violation was punished with exceptional severity. If an agreement had been solemnly made in the presence of the gods, its breach was punishable as an act of gross sacrilege.

III. The third agency for the protection of promises was legal in our sense of the word. It consisted of penalties imposed upon bad faith by the laws of the nation, the rules of the *gens,* or the by-laws of the guild to which the delinquent belonged. What the sanction was in each case we are left to conjecture. It may have been public disgrace, or exclusion from the guild, or the paying of a fine. And as some promises might be strengthened by an appeal to the gods, so might others by an invocation of the people as witnesses.

Agreements then might be of three kinds corresponding to the three kinds of sanction. They might consist of (1) an entirely formless compact, (2) a solemn appeal to the gods, or (3) a solemn appeal to the people.

I. A formless compact is called *pactum* in the language of the twelve Tables. It was merely a distinct understanding between parties who trusted to each other's word, and in the infancy of Law it must have been the kind of agreement most generally used in the ordinary business of life. Such agreements are doubtless the oldest of all, since it is almost impossible to conceive of a time when men did not barter acts and promises as freely as they bartered goods and without the accompaniment of any ceremony. Compacts of this sort were protected by the universal respect for *Fides*, and their violation may perhaps have been visited with penalties by the guild or by the *gens*. But intensely religious as the early Romans were, there must have been cases in which conscience was too weak a barrier against fraud, and slight penalties were ineffectual. Fear of the gods had to be reinforced by the fear of man, and self-help was the remedy which naturally suggested itself. In the twelve Tables *pactum* appears in a negative shape, as a compact by performing which retaliation or a law-suit could be avoided[1]. If this compact was broken the offended party pursued his remedy. Similarly where a positive *pactum* was violated, the injured person must have had the option of chastising

[1] Gell. **xx.** 1. 14. Auct. ad Her. **II.** 13. 20.

the delinquent. His revenge might take the form of personal violence, seizure of the other's goods, or the retention of a pawn already in his possession. He could choose his own mode of punishment, but if his adversary proved too strong for him, he doubtless had to go unavenged; whereas if the broken agreement belonged to either of the other classes, the injured party had the whole support of the priesthood or the community at his back, and thus was certain of obtaining satisfaction. It is therefore plain that though formless agreements contained the germ of Contract, they could not have produced a true law of Contract, because by their very nature they lacked binding force. Their sanction depended on the caprice of individuals, whereas the essence of Contract is that the breach of an agreement is punishable in a particular way. A further element was needed, and this was supplied by the invocation of higher powers.

II. At what period the fashion was introduced of confirming promises by an appeal to the gods it would be idle to guess. Originally, it seems, the plain meaning of such appeals was alone considered, and their form was of no importance. But under the influence of custom or of the priesthood, they assumed by degrees a formal character, and it is thus that we find them in our earliest authorities.

Since Religion and Law were both at first the monopoly of the priestly order, and since the religious forms of promise have their counterpart in the customs of Greece and other primitive peoples, whereas the secular forms are peculiarly Roman[1], the religious forms are evidently the older, and formal contract has therefore had a religious origin. *Fides* being a divine thing, the most natural means of confirming a promise was to place it under divine protection. This could be accomplished in two ways, by *iusiurandum* or by *sponsio*, each of which was a solemn declaration placing the promise or agreement under the guardianship of the gods. Each of these forms has a curious history, and as they are the earliest specimens of true Contract, we may discuss them in the next chapter.

III. Another method, and one peculiar to the Romans, which naturally suggested itself for the protection of agreements, was to perform the whole transaction in view of the people. Publicity ensured the fairness of the agreement, and placed its existence beyond dispute. If the transaction was essentially a public matter, such as the official sale of public lands, or the giving out of public contracts, no formality seems ever to have been required, so that even a formless agreement was in that case binding. The same validity could be secured for private contracts by having them publicly witnessed, and the *nexum* was but one application of this principle. In testamentary Law it seems probable that the public will *in comitiis calatis* was also formless, whereas in private the testator could only give effect to his will by formally saying to his fellow-citizens " *testimonium mihi perhibetote.*"

Thus the two elements which turned a bare

[1] See p. 22.

agreement into a contract were religion and publicity. The naked agreements (*pacta*) need not concern us, since their validity as contracts never received complete recognition. But it will be the object of the following pages to show how agreements grew into contracts by being invested with a religious or public dignity, and to trace the subsequent process by which this outward clothing was slowly cast off. Formalism was the only means by which Contract could have risen to an established position, but when that position was fully attained we shall find Contract discarding forms and returning to the state of bare agreement from which it had sprung.

CHAPTER II.

CONTRACTS OF THE REGAL PERIOD.

Art. 1. IVSIVRANDVM is derived by some from *Iouisiurandum*[1], which merely indicates that Jupiter was the god by whom men generally swore. To make an oath was to call upon some god to witness the integrity of the swearer, and to punish him if he swerved from it. This appears from the wording of the oath in Livy[2], where Scipio says: "*Si sciens fallo, tum me, Iuppiter optime maxime, domum familiam remque meam pessimo leto afficias,*" and from the oath upon the *Iuppiter lapis* given by Polybius and Paulus Diaconus, where a man throws down a flint and says: "*Si sciens fallo, tum me Dispiter salua urbe arceque bonis eiiciat, uti ego hunc lapidem.*" A promise accompanied by an oath was simply a unilateral contract under religious sanction. And it would seem that the oath was in fact used for purposes of contract. Cicero remarks[3] that the oath was proved by the language of the XII Tables to have been in former times the most binding form of promise; and since an oath was still morally binding

---

[1] Cf. Apul. *de deo Socr.* 5. [2] XXII. 53.

[3] *Off.* III. 31. 111.

in the time of Cicero, though it had then no legal
force, the point of his remark must be that in
earlier times the oath was legally binding also.
From Dionysius we know that the altar of *Hercules*
(called *Ara Maxima*) was a place at which solemn
compacts (συνθῆκαι) were often made[1], while Plautus
and Cicero inform us that such compacts were
solemnized by grasping the altar and taking an
oath[2]. It would seem probable that the gods were
consulted by the taking of auspices before an
oath was made. Cicero says that even in private
affairs the ancients used to take no step without
asking the advice of the gods[3]; and we may safely
conjecture that whenever a god was called upon to
witness a solemn promise, he was first enquired of,
so that he might have the option of refusing his
assent by giving unfavourable auspices. The terms
of the oath were known as *concepta uerba*, at least
in the later Republic, and like the other forms of the
period they were strictly construed[4]. *Periurium* did
not mean then, as now, false swearing. It meant
the breach of an oath[5], the commission of any act at
variance with the *uerba concepta*[6].

There is some dispute as to what were the exact
consequences of such a breach. Voigt[7] thinks that
it merely entailed excommunication from religious
rites, but Danz[8] is clearly right in maintaining that
its consequences in early times were far more serious ;

[1] Dion. I. 40.   [2] Plaut. *Rud.* 5. 2. 49.   Cic. *Flacc.* 36. 90.
[3] *Div.* 1. 16. 28.   [4] Seru. *ad Aen.* 12. 13.
[5] i.e. *sciens fallere*, Plin. *Paneg.* 64.   Seneca, *Ben.* III. 37. 4.
[6] *Off.* III. 29. 108.   [7] *Ius Nat.* III. 229.   [8] *Röm. RG.* II. § 149.

they amounted in fact to complete outlawry. Cicero says that the *sacratae leges* of the ancients confirmed the validity of oaths. Now a *sacrata lex* was one which declared the transgressor to be *sacer* (i.e. a victim devoted) to some particular god[1], and *sacer* in the so-called laws of Seruius Tullius[2] and in the XII Tables[3] was the epithet of condemnation applied to the undutiful child and the unrighteous patron. So likewise it seems highly probable that the breaker of an oath became *sacer*, and that his punishment, as Cicero hints[4], was usually death. The formula of an oath given by Polybius[5] is more comprehensive than that given by Paulus Diaconus[6], for in it the swearer prays that, if he should transgress, he may forfeit not only the religious but also the civil rights of his countrymen. This shows that the oath-breaker was an utter outcast; in fact, as the gods could not always execute vengeance in person, what they did was to withdraw their protection from the offender and leave him to the punishment of his fellow-men[7]. The drawbacks to this method of contract were the same as those of the old English Law, which made hanging the penalty for a slight theft; the penalty was likely to be out of all proportion to the injury inflicted by a breach of the promise. So awful indeed was it, that no promise of an ordinary kind could well be given in such a dangerous form, and consequently the oath was not available for the

[1] Festus, p. 318, *s.u. sacratae.*   [2] Fest. p. 230, *s.u. plorare.*
[3] Seru. *ad Aen.* 6. 609.   [4] *Leg.* ii. 9. 22.   [5] iii. 25.
[6] p. 114, *s.u. lapidem.*   [7] Liu. v. 11. 16.

common affairs of daily life. The use of the oath
therefore disappeared with the rise of other forms of
binding agreement, the severity of whose remedies
was proportionate to the rights which had been
violated; while at the same time the breaking
of an oath came to be considered as a moral, instead
of a legal, offence, and by the end of the Republic
entailed nothing more serious than disgrace (*dedecus*).
In one instance only did the legal force of the oath
survive. As late as the days of Justinian, the
services due to patrons by their freedmen were still
promised under oath[1]. But the penalty for the
neglect of those services had changed with the
development of the law. At and before the time of
the XII Tables, the freedman who neglected his
patron, like the patron who injured his freedman[2],
no doubt became *sacer*, and was an outlaw fleeing
for his life, as we are told by Dionysius[3]. But in
classical times the heavy religious penalty had
disappeared, and the *iurisiurandi obligatio* was enforced by a special praetorian action, the *actio
operarum*[4]. By the time of Ulpian the effects of
the *iurata operarum promissio* seem indeed to have
been identical with those of the *operarum stipulatio*[5], though the forms of the two were still quite
distinct.

We may then summarise as follows our knowledge
as to this primitive mode of contract:

The form was a verbal declaration on the part of
the promisor, couched in a solemn and carefully

[1] 38 *Dig.* 1. 7.   [2] Seru. *ad Aen.* 6. 609.   [3] II. 10.
[4] 38 *Dig.* 1. 2 and 7.   [5] Cf. 38 *Dig.* 1. 10.

worded[1] formula (*concepta uerba*), wherein he called upon the gods (*testari deos*)[2], to behold his good faith and to punish him for a breach of it.

The sanction was the withdrawal of divine protection, so that the delinquent was exposed to death at the hand of any man who chose to slay him.

The mode of release, if any, does not appear. In classical times it was the *acceptilatio*[3], but this was clearly anomalous and resulted from the similar juristic treatment of *operae promissae* and *operae iuratae.*

Art. 2. SPONSIO. Though the point is contested by high authority, yet it scarcely admits of a doubt that there existed from very early times another form, known as *sponsio,* by which agreements could be made under religious sanction. This method, as Danz has pointed out, was originally connected with the preceding one. It was derived from the stern and solemn compact made under an oath to the gods. But Danz goes too far when he identifies the two, and states that *sponsio* was but another name for the sworn promise[4]. The stages through which the *sponsio* seems to have passed tell a different story. The word is closely connected with σπονδή, σπένδειν, and hence originally meant a pouring out of wine[5], quite distinct from the convivial λοιβὴ or *libatio*[6], so that "libation" is not its proper equivalent. The other derivation given by

---

[1] 38 *Dig.* 1. 7, *fr.* 3. [2] Plaut. *Rud.* 5. 2. 52.
[3] 46 *Dig.* 4. 13. [4] Danz, *Sacr. Schutz,* p. 105.
[5] Festus p. 329 *s. u. spondere.* [6] Leist, *Greco-It. R. G.* p. 464, note o.

Varro[1] and Verrius[2] from *spons*, the will, whence according to Girtanner[3] *sponsio* must have meant a declaration of the will, savours somewhat too strongly of classical etymology.

I. This pouring out of wine, as Leist[4] has shown, was in the Homeric age a constant accompaniment to the conclusion of a sworn compact of alliance (ὅρκια πιστά) between friendly nations. The sacrificial wine seems originally to have added force to the oath by symbolising the blood which would be spilt if the gods were insulted by a breach of that oath. In this then its original form *sponsio* was nothing more than an accessory piece of ceremonial.

II. The second stage was brought about by the omission of the oath and by the use of wine-pouring alone as the principal ceremony in making less important agreements of a private nature. In the Indian *Sutras* for instance a sacrifice of wine is customary at betrothals[5], and comparison shows that the marriage ceremonies of the Romans, in connection with which we find *sponsio* and *sponsalia* applied to the betrothal and *sponsa* to the bride[6], were very like those of other Aryan communities[7]. We may therefore clearly infer that at Rome also there was a time when the pouring out of wine was a part of the marriage-contract; and thus our derivation of the word receives independent confirmation.

III. In the third and last stage *sponsio* meant

[1] *L. L.* VI. 7. 69.   [2] Festus, *s. u. spondere*.   [3] *Stip.* p. 84.
[4] *Greco-It. R. G.* § 60.   [5] Leist, *Alt-Ar. I. Civ.* p. 443.
[6] Gell. IV. 4. Varro, *L. L.* VI. 7. 70.   [7] Leist, *loc. cit.*

nothing more than a particular form of promise, and it is easy to see how this came about. At first the verbal promise took its name from the ceremony of wine-pouring which gave to it binding force; but in course of time this ceremony was left out as taken for granted, and then the promise alone, provided words of style were correctly used, still retained its old uses and its old name. *Sponsio* from being a ceremonial act became a form of words. Such was the final stage of its development.

The importance attached to the use of the words *spondesne?*, *spondeo* in preference to all others[1] thus becomes clear. *Spondesne? spondeo* originally meant " Do you promise by the sacrifice of wine ?" "I do so promise," just as we say, "I give you my oath," when we do not dream of actually taking one.

Another peculiarity of *sponsio*, noticed though not explained by Gaius[2], was the fact that it could be used in one exceptional case to make a binding agreement between Romans and aliens, namely, at the conclusion of a treaty. Gaius expresses surprise at this exception. But if, as above stated, a sacrifice of pure wine ($\sigma\pi o\nu\delta\alpha\grave{\iota}$ $\accentset{}{\alpha}\kappa\rho\eta\tau o\iota$) was one of the early formalities of an international compact ($\accentset{}{o}\rho\kappa\iota\alpha$ $\pi\iota\sigma\tau\acute{\alpha}$), it was natural that the word *spondeo* should survive on such occasions, even after the oath and the wine-pouring had long since vanished.

Sponsio being then a religious act and subsequently a religious formula, its sanctity was doubtless protected by the pontiffs with suitable penalties. What these penalties were we cannot hope to know,

---

[1] Gai. III. 93.   [2] III. 94.

though clearly they were the forerunners of the
penal *sponsio tertiae partis* of the later procedure.
Varro[1] informs us that, besides being used at betrothals the *sponsio* was employed in money (*pecunia*)
transactions. If *pecunia* includes more than money
we may well suppose that cattle and other forms of
property, which could be designated by number and
not by weight, were capable of being promised in
this manner. Indeed it is by no means unlikely[2]
that *nexum* was at one time the proper form for
a loan of money by weight, while *sponsio* was the
proper form for a loan of coined money (*pecunia
numerata*). The making of a *sponsio* for a sum
of money was at all events the distinguishing feature
of the *actio per sponsionem,* and though we cannot
now enter upon the disputed history of that action,
its antiquity will hardly be denied.

The account here given of the origin and early
history of the *sponsio* is so different from the views
taken by many excellent authorities that we must
examine their theories in order to see why they
appear untenable. One great class of commentators
have held that the *sponsio* is not a primitive institution, but was introduced at a date subsequent to the
XII Tables. The adherents of this theory are
afraid of admitting the existence, at so early a period,
of a form of contract so convenient and flexible
as the *sponsio*, and they also attach great weight to
the fact that no mention of *sponsio* occurs in our
fragments of the XII Tables. While it would
doubtless be an anachronism to ascribe to the early

[1] *L. L.* vi. 7. 70.   [2] Karsten, *Stip.* p. 42.

sponsio the actionability and breadth of scope which it had in later times, still it may very well have been sanctioned by religious law, in ways of which nothing can be known unless the pontifical Commentaries of Papirius[1] should some day be discovered. As to the silence of the XII Tables on this subject, we are told by Pomponius that they were intended to define and reform the law rather than to serve as a comprehensive code[2]. Therefore they may well have passed over a subject like *sponsio* which was already regulated by the priesthood. Or, if they did mention it, their provisions on the subject may have been lost, like the provisions as to *iusiurandum*, which we know of only through a casual remark of Cicero's[3].

The early date here attributed to the *sponsio* cannot therefore be disproved by any such negative evidence. Let us see how the case stands with regard to the question of origin.

(*a*) The theory best known in England, owing to its support by Sir H. Maine, is that *sponsio* was a simplified form of *nexum*, in which the ceremonial had fallen away and the *nuncupatio* had alone been left[4]. This explanation is now so utterly obsolete that it is not worth refuting, especially since Mr Hunter's exhaustive criticism[5]. One fact which in itself is utterly fatal to such a theory is that the *nuncupatio* was an assertion requiring no reply[6],

[1] Dion. III. 36.

[2] 1 *Dig*. 2. 2. 4.

[3] *Off*. III. 31. 111.

[4] Maine, *Anc. Law*, p. 326.

[5] Hunter, *Roman Law*, p. 385.

[6] Gai. II. 24.

whereas the essential thing about the *sponsio* was a question coupled with an answer.

(*b*) Voigt follows Girtanner in maintaining that *spondere* signified originally " to declare one's will," and he vaguely ascribes the use of *sponsiones* in the making of agreements to an ancient custom existing at Rome as well as in Latium[1]. He agrees with the view here expressed that the *sponsio* was known prior to the XII Tables, but thinks that before the XII Tables it was neither a contract (which is strictly true if by contract we mean an agreement enforceable by action), nor an act in the law, and that its use as a contract began in the fourth century as a result of Latin influence[2]. In another place[3] he expresses the opinion that its introduction as a contract was due to legislation, and most probably to the *Lex Silia.* The objections to this view are (1) that the etymology is probably wrong, and (2) that the inference drawn as to the original meaning of *spondere* involves us in serious difficulties. An expression of the will can be made by a formless declaration as well as by a formal one. And if a formless agreement be a *sponsio*, as it must be if *sponsio* means any declaration of the will, how are we to explain the formal importance attaching to the use of the particular words "*spondesne? spondeo.*" (3) This view ignores the religious nature of the *sponsio*, which I have endeavoured to establish, and (4) it forgets that *sponsio*, being part of the marriage ceremonial, one of the first subjects

[1] *Röm. RG.* I. p. 42.   [2] *Ib.* p. 43.
[3] *Ius Nat.* §§ 33–4.

to be regulated by the laws of Romulus[1], is most probably one of the oldest Roman institutions. Again (5), as Esmarch has observed[2], the legislative origin of the *sponsio* is a very rash hypothesis. We only know that the *Lex Silia* introduced an improved procedure for matters which were already actionable, and had a new formal contract been created by such a definite act we should almost certainly have been informed of this by the classical writers.

(c) Danz also derives *sponsio* from *spons,* the will; but he takes *spondere* to mean *sua sponte iurare,* and thinks that the original *sponsio* was exactly the same as *iusiurandum,* i.e. nothing more than an oath of a particular kind[3]. His chief argument for this view is to be found in Paulus Diaconus, who gives *consponsor = coniurator.* But why need we suppose that Paulus meant more than to give a synonym? in which case it by no means follows that *spondere = iurare.* For such a statement as that we have absolutely no authority. Moreover, as we saw above, *iusiurandum* was a one-sided declaration on the part of the promisor only. How then could the *sponsio,* consisting as it did of question and answer, have sprung from such a source? especially since the *iusiurandum,* though no longer armed with a legal sanction, was still used as late as the days of Plautus alongside of the *sponsio* and in complete contrast to it?

(d) Girtanner, in his reply to the "Sacrale Schutz" of Danz[4], maintains that *sponsio* had nothing

<hr />

[1] Dion. ii. 25.

[2] *K. V. für G. u. R. W.* ii. 516.

[3] *Sacr. Schutz,* p. 149.

[4] *Ueber die Sponsio,* p. 4 ff.

to do with an oath, but was a simple declaration of
the individual will, and that *stipulatio* had its origin
in the respect paid to *Fides*. This view however
is even less supported by evidence than that of
Danz[1]. Arguing again from analogy Girtanner
thinks that, as the Roman people regulated its
affairs by expressing its will publicly in the *Comitia*,
so we may conjecture that individuals could validly
express their will in private affairs, in other words
could make a binding *sponsio*. But this, as well
as being a wrong analogy, is a misapprehension of a
leading principle of early Law. For, as we have
seen, no agreement resting simply upon the will of
the parties (i.e. *pactum*) was valid without some
outward stamp being affixed to it, in the shape
of approval expressed by the gods or by the people.
In the language of the more modern law, we may
say that such approval, tacit or explicit, religious or
secular, was the original *causa ciuilis* which distinguished *contractus* from *pactiones*. Now a popular
vote in the *Comitia* bore the stamp of public
approval as plainly as did the *nexum*. But the
sponsio, requiring no witnesses, was clearly not
endorsed by the people; therefore the endorsement
which it needed in order to become a *contractus
iuris ciuilis* must have been of a religious nature,
and that such was the case appears plainly if we
admit that *sponsio* originated in a religious ceremonial such as I have described.

To recapitulate the view here given, we may
conclude that *sponsio* was a primordial institution

[1] See Windscheid, *K. V. für G. u. R. W.* I. 291.

of the Roman and Latin peoples, which grew into its later form through three stages. (*a*) It was originally a sacrifice of wine annexed to a solemn compact of alliance or of peace made under an oath to the gods. (*b*) Next it became a sacrifice used as an appeal to the gods in compacts not made under oath such as betrothals. Just as *iusiurandum* for many purposes was sufficient without the pouring out of wine, so for other purposes *sponsio* came to be sufficient without the oath. (*c*) Lastly it became a verbal formula, expressed in language implying the accompaniment of a wine-sacrifice, but at the making of which no sacrifice was ever actually performed. In this final stage, which continued as late as the days of Justinian,

Its form was a question put by the promisee, and an answer given by the promisor, each using the verb *spondere*. " *Filiam mihi spondesne ?* " " *Spondeo.*" " *Centum dari spondes ?* " " *Spondeo.*" Throughout its history this was a form which Roman citizens alone could use, in which fact we clearly see religious exclusiveness and a further proof of religious origin. Why they used question and answer rather than plain statement is a minor point the origin of which no theory has yet accounted for. The most plausible conjecture seems to be that the recapitulation by the promisee was intended to secure the complete understanding by the promisor of the exact nature of his promise.

Its sanction in the early period of which we are treating was doubtless imposed by the priests, but owing to our almost complete ignorance of the pontifical law we cannot tell what that sanction was.

Having now examined the ways in which an agreement could be made binding under religious sanction, let us see how binding agreements could be made with the approval of the community. There is reason to believe that this secular class of contracts is less ancient than the religious class, because *nexum* and *mancipium* were peculiar to the Romans, whereas traces of *iusiurandum* and *sponsio* are found, as Leist has shown, in other Aryan civilizations[1].

Art. 3. NEXVM. There is no more disputed subject in the whole history of Roman Law than the origin and development of this one contract. Yet the facts are simple, and though we cannot be sure that every detail is accurate, we have enough information to see clearly what the transaction was like as a whole. We know that it was a *negotium per aes et libram*, a weighing of raw copper or other commodity measured by weight in the presence of witnesses[2]; that the commodity so weighed was a loan[3]; and that default in the repayment of a loan thus made exposed the borrower to bondage[4] and savage punishment at the hands of the lender. We know also that it existed as a loan before the XII Tables, for it is mentioned in them as something quite different from *mancipium*[5]. To assert, as Bechmann does, that since *nexum* included conveyance as

---

[1] *Alt Ar. I. Civ. I^te Abt.* pp. 435–443.
[2] Gai. III. 173. [3] *Mucius* in Varro, *L. L.* 7. 105.
[4] Varro, *L. L.* VI. 5. [5] Clark, *E. R. L.* § 22.

well as loan "*mancipiumque*" must therefore be an
interpolation into the text of the XII Tables[1], is an
arbitrary and unnecessary conjecture. The etymology
of *nexum* and of *mancipium* shows that they were
distinct conceptions. *Mancipium* implies the transfer
of *manus*, ownership; *nexum* implies the making of
a bond (*cf. nectere*, to bind), the precise equivalent
of *obligatio* in the later law. It is true that both
nexum and *mancipium* required the use of copper
and scales, to measure in one case the price, in the
other the amount of the loan. But this coincidence
by no means proves that the two transactions were
identical. A modern deed is used both for leases and
for conveyances of real property, yet that would be
a strange argument to prove that a lease and a
conveyance were originally the same thing. Here
however we are met by a difficulty. If, as some
hold[2] and as I have tried to prove, we must regard
mancipium as an institution of prehistoric times
distinct from the purely contractual *nexum*, how
are we to explain the fact that *nexum* is used
by Cicero[3] and by other classical writers[4] as equivalent to *mancipium*, or as a general term signifying
omne quod per aes et libram geritur, whether a loan,
a will, or a conveyance ? Now first we must notice
the fact that *nexum* had at any rate not always been
synonymous with *mancipium*, for if it had been so,
there could have been no doubt in the minds of

[1] *Kauf*, p. 130.   [2] Mommsen, *Hist.* 1. 11. p. 162 n.

[3] *ad Fam.* 7. 30 ; *de Or.* 3. 40 ; *Top.* 5. 28 ; *Parad.* 5. 1. 35. ; *pro
Mur.* 2.

[4] Boethius *lib.* 3 *ad Top.* 5. 28 ; *Gallus Aelius* in Festus, *s.u.
nexum* ; *Manilius* in Varro, *L. L.* 7. 105.

Scaeuola and Varro that a *res nexa* was the same thing as a *res mancipata*. This Scaeuola and Varro both deny, and we must remember that Mucius Scaeuola was the Papinian of his day. Manilius[1] on the other hand, struck perhaps by the likeness in form of the obsolete *nexum* to other still existing *negotia per aes et libram,* seems to have made *nexum* into a generic term for this whole class of transactions. In this he was followed by Gallus Aelius[2]. The new and wider meaning, given by them to that which was a technical term at the period of the XII Tables, apparently became general in literature, partly for the very reason that *nexum* no longer had an actual existence, partly because *nexi liberatio,* the old release of *nexum,* had been adopted by custom as the proper form of release in matters which had nothing to do with the original *nexum,* namely in the release of judgment-debts and of legacies *per damnationem*[3]. One peculiarity mentioned by Gaius in the release of such legacies seems altogether fatal to the theory that *mancipium* was but a species of the genus *nexum.* Gaius says that *nexi liberatio* could be used only for legacies of things measured by weight. Such things were the sole objects of the true *nexum,* whereas *res mancipi* included land and cattle. Therefore if *mancipium* were only a species of *nexum* we should certainly find *nexi liberatio* applying to legacies of *res mancipi,* but this, as Gaius shows, was not the case.

The view that *nexum* was the parent *gestum per*

---

[1] Varro, *L. L.* vii. 105.   [2] Festus, p. 165, *s. u. nexum.*

[3] Gai. iii. 173–5.

aes et libram, and that *mancipium* was the name given later to one particular form of *nexum,* is worth examining at some length, because it is widely accepted[1], and because it fundamentally affects our opinion concerning the early history of an important contract. Bechmann[2] thinks it more reasonable to suppose that *nexum* narrowed from a general to a specific conception. But it is scarcely conceivable that *nexum* should have had the vague generic meaning of *quodcumque per aes et libram geritur*[3] when it was still a living mode of contract, and the technical meaning of *obligatio per aes et libram* when such a contractual form no longer existed. What seems far more likely is that *nexum* had a technical meaning until it ceased to be practised subsequently to the *Lex Poetilia,* and that its loose meaning was introduced in the later Republic, partly to denote the binding force of any contract[4], partly as a convenient expression for any transaction *per aes et libram*[5]. Even in Cicero we find the word *nexum* used chiefly with a view to elegance of style[6] in places where *mancipatio* would have been a clumsy word and where[7] there could be no doubt as to the real meaning. But when Cicero is writing history, he uses *nexum* in its old technical sense and actually tells us that it had become obsolete[8].

[1] See Bechmann, *Kauf,* I. p. 130 ; Clark, *E. R. L.* § 22.
[2] *Ib.* p. 131.   [3] Varro, *l. c.*—Festus, *s. u. nexum.*
[4] Cf. "*nexu uenditi*" in Ulpian, 12 *Dig.* 6. 26. 7.
[5] Cic. *de Or.* III. 40. 159.
[6] *Har. Resp.* VII. 14 ; *ad Fam.* VII. 30. 2 ; *Top.* 5. 28.
[7] As in *pro Mur.* 2 ; *Parad.* v. 1. 35.
[8] *de Rep.* 2. 34 and cf. Liu. VIII. 28. 1.

Rejecting then as untenable the notion that *nexum* denoted a variety of transactions, let us see how it originated. The most obvious way of lending corn or copper or any other ponderable commodity, was to weigh it out to the borrower, who would naturally at the same time specify by word of mouth the terms on which he accepted the loan. In order to make the transaction binding, an obvious precaution would be to call in witnesses, or if the transaction took place, as it most likely would, in the market-place, the mere publicity of the loan would be enough. Thus it was, we may believe, that a *nexum* was originally made. It was a formless agreement necessarily accompanied by the act of weighing and made under public supervision. It dealt only with commodities which could be measured with the scales and weights, and did not recognize the distinction between *res mancipi* and *res nec mancipi*,—a strong argument that *nexum* and *mancipium* were, as above said, totally distinct affairs. Its sanction lay in the acts of violence which the creditor might see fit to commit against the debtor, if payment was not performed according to the terms of his agreement. Personal violence was regulated by the XII Tables, in the rules of *manus iniectio*, but before that time it is safe to conjecture that any form of retaliation against the person or property of the debtor was freely allowed.

The fixing of the number of witnesses at five[1], which we find also in *mancipium*, is the only modification of *nexum* that we know of prior to

[1] Gai. III. 174.

the XII Tables. Bekker[1] suggests that this change
was one of the reforms of Seruius Tullius, and that
the five witnesses, by representing the five classes of
the Servian *census*, personified the whole people.
This is a mere conjecture, but a very plausible one.
For we are told by Dionysius[2] that Seruius made
fifty enactments on the subject of Contract and
Crime, and in another passage of the same author[3],
we find an analogous case of a law which forbade the
exposure of a child except with the approval of five
witnesses. But here a question has been raised as to
what the witnesses did. The correct answer, I
believe, is that given by Bechmann[4], who maintains
that the witnesses approved the transaction as a
whole, and vouched for its being properly and fairly
performed. Huschke, on the other hand, claims that
the function of the witnesses was to superintend the
weighing of the copper, and that before the introduction of coined money some such public supervision
was necessary in order to convert the raw copper
into a lawful medium of exchange[5]. This view
is part of Huschke's theory, that *nexum* had two
marked peculiarities: (1) it was a legal act performed under public authority, and (2) it was the
recognised mode of measuring out copper money by
weight.

The first part of Huschke's theory may be
accepted without reserve, but the second part seems
quite untenable. We have no evidence to show
that *nexum* was confined to loans of money or of

[1] *Akt.* I. 22 ff.   [2] IV. 13.   [3] II. 15.
[4] *Kauf*, I. p. 90.   [5] *Nexum*, p. 16 ff.

copper. Indeed we gather from a passage of Cicero
that *far*, corn, may have been the earliest object of
nexum[1], while Gaius states that *anything* measurable
by weight could be dealt with by *nexi solutio*[2]. No
inference in favour of Huschke's theory can be
drawn from the name *negotium per aes et libram*,
for this phrase obviously dates from the more recent
times when the ceremony had only a formal significance, and when the *aes* (*raudusculum*) was merely
struck against the scales. If then we reject the
second part of Huschke's theory, and admit, as
we certainly should, that *nexum* could deal with any
ponderable commodity, it is evident that his whole
view as to the function of the witnesses must
collapse also. The very notion of turning copper
from merchandise into legal tender is far too subtle
to have ever occurred to the minds of the early
Romans. As Bechmann[3] rightly remarks, the
original object of the State in making coin was
not to create an authorised medium of exchange,
but simply to warrant the weight and fineness of
the medium most generally used. The view of
Huschke seems therefore a complete anachronism.

There is also another interpretation of *nexum*
radically different from the one here advocated, and
formerly given by some authorities[4], but which
has few if any supporters among modern jurists.
This view was founded upon a loosely expressed
remark of Varro's in which *nexus* is defined as

---

[1] Cic. *de Leg. Agr*. II. 30. 83.   [2] III. 175.   [3] *Kauf*, I. p. 87.

[4] See Sell, Scheurl, Niebuhr, Christiansen, Puchta, quoted in
Danz, *Röm. RG*. II. 25.

a freeman who gives himself into slavery for a debt
which he owes[1]. The inference drawn from this
remark was that the debtor's body, not the creditor's
money, was the object of *nexum*, and that a debtor
who sold himself by *mancipium* as a pledge for the
repayment of a loan was said to make a *nexum*[2].
Such a theory does not however harmonize with the
facts. The evidence is entirely opposed to it, for
Varro's statement, as will be seen later on, admits of
quite another meaning. Neither *nexum* nor *mancipium* is ever found practised by a man upon
his own person. Nor could *nexum* have applied to a
debtor's person, for the idea of treating a debtor like
a *res mancipi* or like a thing *quod pondere numero
constat*, is absurd. Again, if *nexum = mancipium*, the
conveyance of the debtor's body as a pledge must
have taken effect as soon as the money was lent,
therefore (1) by thus becoming *nexus* he must have
been *in mancipio* long before a default could occur,
which is too strange to be believed, and (2) being *in
mancipio* he must have been *capite deminutus*[3], which
Quintilian expressly states that no nexal debtor ever
was[4]. Clearly then *mancipium* was under no circumstances a factor in *nexum*.

Thus it would seem that the theory which
regards *nexum* as a loan of raw copper or other goods
measurable by weight, is the one beset with fewest
difficulties. Such goods correspond pretty nearly
to what in the later law were called *res fungibiles*.

---

[1] Varro, *L. L.* vii. 105 and see page 52.
[2] *nexum inire*, Liu. vii. 19. 5.
[3] Paul. Diac. p. 70, *s. u. deminutus*.   [4] *Decl.* 311.

The borrower was not required to return the very same thing, but an equal quantity of the same kind of thing. And this explains why *nexum*, the first genuine contract of the Roman Law, should have received such ample protection. A tool or a beast of burden could be lent with but little risk, for either could be easily identified; but the loan of corn or of metal would have been attended with very great risk, had not the law been careful to ensure the publicity of every such transaction. *Iusiurandum* or *sponsio* might no doubt have been used for making loans, but they both lacked the great advantage of accurate measurement, which *nexum* owed to its public character. It was the presence of witnesses which raised *nexum* from a formless loan into a contract of loan.

This general sketch of the original *nexum* is all that can be given with certainty. The details of the picture cannot be filled in, unless we draw upon our imagination. We do not know what verbal agreement passed between the borrower and the lender, though it is fairly certain that payment of interest on the loan might be made a part of the contract. We cannot even be quite sure whether the scale-holder (*libripens*) was an official, as some have suggested, or a mere assistant[1].

Our description of the contract may then be briefly recapitulated as follows:

The form consisted of the weighing out and delivery to the borrower of goods measurable by weight, in the presence of witnesses, (five in number,

[1] See page 52.

probably since the time of Seruius Tullius), whose
attendance ensured the proper performance of the
ceremony. The ownership of the particular goods
passed to the borrower, who was merely bound to
return an equal quantity of the same kind of goods,
but the terms of each contract were approximately
fixed by a verbal agreement uttered at the time.

The sanction consisted of the violent measures
which the creditor might choose to take against a
defaulting debtor. Before the XII Tables there
seems to have been no limit to the creditor's power
of punishment. Any violence against the debtor
was approved by custom and justified by the noto-
riety of the transaction, so that self-help was more
easily exercised and probably more severe in the case
of *nexum* than in that of any other agreement.

The release (nexi solutio) was a ceremony precisely similar to that of the *nexum* itself, the amount
of the loan being weighed and delivered to the lender,
in presence of witnesses[1].

Art. 4. We have now examined three methods
by which a binding promise could be made in the
earliest period of the Roman Law. The next
question which confronts us is whether there existed
at that time any other method. The other forms of
contract, besides those already described, which are
found existing at the period of the XII Tables, were
fiducia, lex mancipi, uadimonium, and *dotis dictio.*
Did any of these have their origin before this time?
Fiducia is doubtful, and *lex mancipi,* as we shall
see, owed its existence to an important provision

---

[1] Gai. III. 174.

of that code. As to the origin of *uadimonium*, we cannot be certain, but judging from a passage in Gellius[1] we are almost forced to the conclusion that *uadimonium* also was a creation of the XII Tables. Gellius speaks of "*uades et subuades et XXV asses et taliones...omnisque illa XII Tabularum antiquitas.*" We know that twenty-five asses was the fine imposed by the XII Tables for cutting down another man's tree, therefore it would seem from the context that *uades* had also been introduced by that code. The point cannot be settled, but since the XII Tables were at any rate the first enactments on the subject of which anything is known, we may discuss *uadimonium* in treating of the next period. The only contract of which the remote antiquity is beyond dispute is the *dotis dictio*.

Art. 5. DOTIS DICTIO. Dionysius[2] informs us that in the earliest times a dowry was given with daughters on their marriage, and that if the father could not afford this expense his clients were bound to contribute. Hence it is clear not only that *dos* existed from very early times, but that custom even in remote antiquity had fenced it about with strict rules. From Ulpian[3] we know that *dos* could be bestowed either by *dotis dictio, dotis promissio,* or *dotis datio.* The *promissio* was a promise by stipulation, and the *datio* was the transfer by mancipation or tradition of the property constituting the dowry; so that these two are easy to understand. But *dotis dictio* is an obscure subject. It is difficult to know whence it acquired its binding force as a contract,

[1] XVI. 10. 8.   [2] II. 10.   [3] *Reg.* VI. 1.

since in form it was unlike all other contracts
with which we are acquainted. Its antiquity is
evidenced not only by this peculiarity of form, but
also by a passage in the Theodosian Code which
speaks of *dotis dictio* as conforming with the ancient
law[1]. An illustration occurs in Terence[2], where the
father says, "*Dos, Pamphile, est decem talenta*,"
and Pamphilus, the future son-in-law, replies,
"*Accipio*"; but we need not conclude that the
transaction was always formal, for the above Code[3],
in permitting the use of any form, seems rather
to be restating the old law than making a new
enactment. A further peculiarity, stated by Ulpian[4]
and by Gaius[5], was that *dotis dictio* could be validly
used only by the bride, by her father or cognates on
the father's side, or by a debtor of the bride acting
with her authority. *Dictio* is a significant word, for
Ulpian[6] distinguishes between *dictum* and *promis-
sum*, the former, he says, being a mere statement,
the latter a binding promise. This distinction should
doubtless be applied in the present case, since *dotis
dictio* and *dotis promissio* were clearly different.

The following theories seem to be erroneous:

(*a*) Von Meykow[7] holds that *dictio* was adopted
as a form of promise instead of *sponsio* for this family
affair of *dos*, in order not to hurt the feelings of the
bride and of her kinsmen by appearing to question
their *bona fides*. That theory would be a plausible
explanation, if *dictio* could ever have meant a

---

[1] *C. Th.* 3. 12. 3.   [2] *And.* 5. 4. 48.   [3] 3. 13. 4.
[4] *Reg.* VI. 2.   [5] *Epit.* II. 9. 3.   [6] 21 *Dig.* 1. 19.
[7] *Dict. d. Röm. Brautg.* p. 5 ff.

promise, but from what Ulpian says, this can hardly be admitted.

(b) Bechmann[1], again, connects *dotis dictio* with the ceremony of *sponsio* at the betrothal of a daughter. The *dos*, he thinks, was promised by a *sponsio* made at the betrothal, so that the peculiar form known as *dotis dictio* was originally nothing more than the specification of a dowry already promised. The *dotis dictio* would therefore have been at first a mere *pactum adiectum*, which was made actionable in later times, while still preserving its ancient form. The objection to this theory is that it lacks evidence : indeed the only passage (that of Terence) in which *dotis dictio* is presented to us with a context goes to show that this contract was in no way connected with the act of betrothal.

(c) Another explanation is given by Czylharz[2], i.e. that *dotis dictio* was a formal contract. His view is based on the *scholia* attached to the passage of Terence, which say of the bridegroom's answer : "*ille nisi dixisset ' accipio' dos non esset.*" Czylharz therefore looks upon the contract as an inverted stipulation. The offer of a promise was made by the promisor, and when accepted by the promisee became a contract. Though such a process is quite in harmony with modern notions of Contract, it would have been a complete anomaly at Rome. And we cannot believe that, if acceptance by the promisee had been a necessary part of the *dotis dictio*, we should not have been so informed by Gaius, when he has been so careful to impress

---

[1] *Röm. Dotalrecht.* 2 Abt. p. 103.   [2] *Z. f. R. G.* VII. 243.

upon us that the *dotis dictio* could be made *nulla interrogatione praecedente.* Thus the view of Czylharz besides being in itself improbable is almost entirely unsupported by evidence. Even the scholiast on Terence need not necessarily mean that "*accipio*" was an indispensable part of the transaction. He may merely have meant that the bridegroom at this juncture could decline the proffered *dos* if he chose, and this interpretation is borne out by Iulianus[1] and Marcellus[2], who give formulæ of *dotis dictio* without any words of acceptance.

A satisfactory solution of the problem seems to have been found by Danz[3]. He looks upon *dos* as having been due from the father or male ascendants of the bride as an *officium pietatis*[4], and quotes passages from the classical writers in which they speak of refusing to dower a sister or a daughter as a most shameful thing[5]. The source of the obligation lay in this relationship to the bride, not in any binding effect of the *dotis dictio* itself. But in order that the obligation might be actionable its amount had to be fixed, and this was just what the *dictio* accomplished. It was an acknowledgment of the debt which custom had decreed that the bride's family must pay to the bridegroom. In this respect the *dos* was precisely analogous to the debt of service which a freedman owed as an *officium* to his patron, and which he acknowledged by the *iurata operarum promissio.* The *dos* and the *operae* were both *officia pietatis,* but

---

[1] 23 *Dig.* 3. 44.   [2] 23 *Dig.* 3. 59.   [3] *Röm. RG.* I. 163.
[4] See 23 *Dig.* 3. 2.   [5] Plaut. *Trin.* 3. 2. 63 ; Cic. *Quint.* 31. 98.

it became customary to specify their nature and their quantity. In the one case this was done by an oath, in the other by a simple declaration, and in both cases the law gave an action to protect these anomalous forms of agreement. What kind of action could be brought on a *dotis dictio* is not known. Voigt[1] states it to have been an *actio dictae dotis,* for which he even gives the formula, but formula and action are alike purely conjectural. We can only infer that the *dotis dictio* was actionable since it constituted a valid contract. How or when this came to pass we cannot tell.

A further advantage of Danz' theory, and one not mentioned by him, is that it explains the capacity of the three classes of persons by whom alone *dotis dictio* could be performed. (1) The father and male ascendants of the bride were bound to provide a *dos* under penalty of *ignominia*[2]; (2) the bride, if *sui iuris,* was bound to contribute to the support of her husband's household for exactly the same reason[3]; and (3) a debtor of the bride was bound to carry out her orders with respect to her assets in his possession, and supposing her whole fortune to have consisted of a debt due to her, it is evident that a *dotis dictio* by the debtor was the only way in which this fortune could be settled as a *dos* at all. Thus the hypothesis that the *dos* was a debt morally due from the father of the bride, or from the bride herself, whenever a marriage took place, completely explains the curious limitation with

[1] *XII Taf.* II. § 123.   [2] 24 *Dig.* 3. 1.   [3] Cic. *Top.* 4. 23.

regard to the parties who could perform *dotis dictio*. The nature of the transaction may then be summarized as follows :

Its form was an oral declaration on the part of (1) the bride's father or male cognates, (2) of the bride herself, or (3) of a debtor of the bride, setting forth the nature and amount of the property which he or she meant to bestow as dowry, and spoken in the presence of the bridegroom. Land as well as moveables could be settled in this manner[1]. No particular formula was necessary. The bridegroom might, if he liked, express himself satisfied with the *dos* so specified ; but his acceptance does not seem to have been an essential feature of the proceeding. Most probably he did not have to speak at all.

Its sanction does not appear, though we may be sure that there was some action to compel performance of the promise. This action, whatever it may have been, could of course be brought by the bride's husband against the maker of the *dotis dictio*. Perhaps in the earliest times the sanction was a purely religious one.

Art. 6. Now that we have seen the various ways in which a binding contract could be made in the earliest period of Roman history, we may consider briefly the general characteristics of that primitive contractual system. The first striking point is that all the contracts hitherto mentioned are unilateral : the promisor alone was bound, and he was not entitled, in virtue of the contract, to any counterperformance on the part of the promisee.

[1] Gai. *Ep.* 3. 9.

The second point is that the consent of the parties was not sufficient to bind them. Over and above that consent the agreement between them was required to bear the stamp of popular or divine approval. Even in *dotis dictio*, as we have just seen, a simple declaration uttered by the promisor was invested with the force of a contract merely because the substance of that declaration was a transfer of property approved and required by public opinion. Thirdly we notice that the intention of the contracting parties was verbally expressed, but that the language employed was not originally of any importance (except in the one case of *sponsio*), provided the intention was clearly conveyed. We must therefore modify the statement so commonly made that the earliest known contracts were couched in a particular form of words. For how did each of these particular forms originate and acquire the shape in which we afterwards find it? By having long been used to express agreements which were binding though their language was informal, and by having thus gradually obtained a technical significance. Consequently the formal stage was not the earliest stage of Contract. The most primitive contract of all was not an agreement clothed with a form, but an agreement clothed with the approval of Church or State.

CHAPTER III.

THE TWELVE TABLES.

Art. 1. THE causes leading to the enactment of the great Reform Bill known as the XII Tables were chiefly social, and the indefinite state of the law was the grievance which called most loudly for a remedy. Contracts and conveyances were but little respected, the powers of the nexal creditor were sorely abused, and legal procedure in general was most uncertain. Yet more than all else the law of torts and crimes needed radical reform: so that though we possess but few actual fragments of the XII Tables we have enough to tell us that very little space was devoted to reforms in the law of Contract. This fact ought not to surprise us, knowing as we do that commerce was still in a very backward state.

We hear nothing of any provision in the XII Tables with respect to *sponsio*, but we know from Cicero that *iusiurandum* was recognised and enforced[1]. *Dotis dictio* was not mentioned, so far as we can discover. A new form, the *lex mancipi*,

---

[1] *Off.* III. 31. 111.

was created by one provision of this code, though its creation was not apparently intended by the Decemvirs, but was rather the result of juristic interpretation. *Vadimonium,* a contract which we have not yet examined, was either created or considerably modified by the XII Tables, and constituted the earliest form of suretyship.

As the hard condition of nexal debtors was one of the evils which led most directly to the secession of the *plebs* and to the consequent enactment of the new code, we should naturally expect to find laws passed for their protection. Accordingly it is with *nexum* that the contractual clauses of the XII Tables are principally concerned.

Art. 2. NEXVM. I. The first provision as to this contract was embodied in the famous words which Festus has transmitted to us: CVM NEXVM FACIET MANCIPIVMQVE VTI LINGVA NVNCVPASSIT ITA IVS ESTO[1]. This was equivalent to saying that the language used by the party making a *nexum* was to be strictly followed in determining what his rights and liabilities should be. The fact that such a declaratory law was needed discloses two features of the primitive *nexum.* We can see (1) that the act of weighing, not the words which accompanied that act, was the essence of the original transaction, so that the scales must have been used actually, and not symbolically as they were in later days: (2) that the terms of a nexal loan must often have been disobeyed; if, for instance,

[1] Festus, p. 171, *s. u. nuncupata pecunia.*

CHANGES IN *NEXVM.* **41**

the debtor had agreed to pay at the end of one year, it might happen that a harsh creditor would enforce payment at the end of six months. This shows that the people were not feared as witnesses to the same extent as were the gods who presided over *iusiurandum* and *sponsio.* The fact of the loan was proved beyond question by the witnesses present, but there was evidently no sacred virtue in the words which went with the loan, and these were not therefore binding simply because spoken in the people's hearing. This defect was what the XII Tables aimed at correcting. They thenceforth placed the verbal terms of *nexum* on as strong a footing as the words of *sponsio.* Conditions as to the amount of interest payable, the date of maturity of the loan, the security to be given by the debtor, could all now be inserted in the verbal *nuncupatio.* And still more important was the fact that the sum or amount of the loan itself could be verbally announced at the ceremony, so that if the debtor said "I hereby receive and am bound to repay fifty *asses,*" this speech was as binding upon him as if the fifty *asses* had been actually weighed out to him in copper. As long as the money or corn was really weighed in the scales, *nexum* continued to be a natural and material method of loan; but when by the introduction of coined money it became possible to count instead of weighing a given quantity of copper, then *nexum* tended to become an artificial and symbolical operation. The reason obviously is that counting is far more simple than weighing. Thus when a loan of 100 *asses* was being made,

it became customary to name this sum in the
nuncupatio without weighing it at all. The scales
and witnesses appeared as before, but the scales
were not used. The borrower, instead of taking 100
asses out of the scale-pan, simply struck it with a
piece of copper so as to conform with the outward
semblance of the transaction. Though the weighing
had been dispensed with, yet by this rule of the
XII Tables he was as much bound in the sum of
100 *asses* as though they had actually been weighed
out to him. Hence the important effect of the
clause which I have quoted. Given a proper coinage
that clause transformed the loan of money into
a *datio imaginaria* and the release of such a loan
into an *imaginaria solutio*. The outward form of
nexum remained the same, but the actual process
was greatly simplified. This change was doubtless
not intended when the rule was made by the
Decemvirs. It was the result of a more or less
unconscious and probably gradual development.
The genuine weighing and the fictitious weighing
doubtless existed side by side. But it seems fairly
certain that the introduction of coined money was
another of the Decemviral reforms[1], and if so, we may
assume that *nexum* changed from a ceremony
performed with the scales into one performed with
copper and scales (*negotium per aes et libram*) not
long after the Decemviral legislation.

II. Another important provision relating to
nexum modified the harsh remedy hitherto applied
by the creditor against the delinquent debtor.

[1] Mommsen, *Röm. Münzw.* p. 175.

RESTRICTIONS ON POWER OF CREDITOR.

The words of the XII Tables have been fortu-
nately preserved by Gellius[1], and run as follows:
AERIS CONFESSI REBVSQVE IVRE IVDICATIS XXX DIES
IVSTI SVNTO. POST DEINDE MANVS INIECTIO ESTO.
IN IVS DVCITO. NI IVDICATVM FACIT AVT QVIS ENDO
EO IN IVRE VINDICIT SECVM DVCITO VINCITO AVT
NERVO AVT COMPEDIBVS XV PONDO NE MINORE AVT
SI VOLET MAIORE VINCITO. SI VOLET SVO VIVITO.
NI SVO VIVIT QVI EVM VINCTVM HABEBIT LIBRAS
FARRIS ENDO DIES DATO. SI VOLET PLVS DATO.
There are two knotty points in the above passage.
(1) What is the exact distinction between ac-
knowledged money debts (*aes confessum*) and judg-
ments obtained by regular process of Law (*res iure
iudicatae*)? (2) To what class of delinquents did
the punishment apply?

(1) It can hardly be doubted[2] that *aes confessum* included a debt contracted by *nexum*, as
well as any other kind of debt the existence of which
was not denied by the debtor. For example, a
debt incurred by formless agreement or by *sponsio*
would be an instance of *aes confessum*, provided
the debtor admitted his liability. But in *nexum*
this liability had already been admitted solemnly
and before witnesses; to deny the existence of a
nexal debt was impossible. Therefore *aes confessum* seems to be a term quite applicable to a
debt contracted by *nexum*. The words *aeris nexi*
were probably not used in the context because
aeris confessi had a wider meaning, and this law

---

[1] xx. 1. 45.   [2] Ihering, *G. d. R. R.* I. 156, note.

was apparently intended to cover much more than the one case of nexal indebtedness.

The other class of debts here described as *res iure iudicatae* are no doubt judgment-debts. Where damages had been judicially awarded to one of the parties to an action, some means had to be provided of compelling payment from the other party. The executive in those early times was too weak to enforce its decisions, and self-help, as we have seen, was the usual resource of aggrieved persons. The only way in which the law could assist judgment creditors was by declaring what extent of retaliation they might lawfully take. And this brings us to the second question :

(2) In what cases was the above mentioned *manus iniectio* to be exercised ? Voigt[1] remarks that the XII Tables never mention *manus iniectio* as being a means of punishing default in a case of *nexum*. He then proceeds to state that the remedy for *nexum* was an *actio pecuniae nuncupatae*. Not only is this statement purely fanciful, as there is no mention of *actio pecuniae nuncupatae* in any of our authorities, but Voigt has surely ignored the evidence before him. Admitting, as we must, that *nexum* is included among the cases named at the beginning of the above clause, we can scarcely avoid the further conclusion long ago reached by Huschke that the rest of the clause, with its 30 days of grace, *manus iniectio, ductio in ius*, and all the consequences of disregarding the *iudicatum*, is a description of the punishment to which a breach of

[1] *XII Taf.* I. 169.

nexum might lead, as well as of that annexed to the other kinds of *aes confessum* and to *res iure iudicatae*. The whole clause is one continuous statement, and to hold that the latter part of it, beginning at NI IVDICATVM FACIT, provides a penalty solely for the case of judgment-debts, seems a very strained and unnatural interpretation. Why explain *iudicatum* as referring only to judgment indebtedness? Just before it in the text we find the direction IN IVS DVCITO, so that a nexal debtor after *manus iniectio* evidently had to be brought into court. The precaution was probably a new restraint upon the violence of creditors, in order that the justice of their claims and the propriety of *manus iniectio* might be judicially determined. But if a judge had to pronounce upon the validity of such proceedings, surely his decree might be described by the term *iudicatum*, as found in the above passage. It is no answer to say that the nature of *aes confessum* precludes the possibility of a judicial decision, and that therefore *iudicatum* can only refer to a *res iure iudicata*, that is, a judgment-debt. For in spite of this alleged distinction we find here that debtors of *aes confessum* and judgment-debtors were treated in exactly the same way. Each of them was at first seized by his creditor and brought into court. Now why should this have been necessary in the case of a *iudicatus* more than in that of a *nexus*? For a judgment-debt seems to need judicial recognition just as little as a nexal debt. And yet we find that *ductio in ius* was prescribed in both cases. The only

rational way of explaining the difficulty, seems
to be to take *iudicatum* in the sense not of a
judgment-debt but of a judicial decree, and to
translate the passage as follows: " Let the creditor
bring the debtor into court. Unless the debtor
obeys the decree of the court or finds meanwhile
a champion of his cause[1] in the court, let the
creditor lead him off into private custody, and
fetter him " etc. etc. Thus the *ductio in ius*, the
iudicatum, the *domum ductio*, and the directions as
to the right kind of fetters and the proper quantity
of food, must all have applied equally to *aes confessum* (including *nexum*) and to *res iure iudicatae*.
This view is confirmed by the passage in which
Livy[2] describes the abolition of the severe penalties
of *nexum*. The bill by which this was done or-
dained, so Livy tells us, " *nequis, nisi qui noxam
meruisset, donec poenam lueret, in compedibus aut in
neruo teneretur...ita nexi soluti, cautumque in pos-
terum ne necterentur.*" This law, the *Lex Poetilia*,
was evidently passed for the relief of *nexi*, and
relief was given by abolishing the use of *compedes
et neruum*. Now as this was the very description of
fetters given by the XII Tables in our text, it
seems certain that the language of the *Lex Poetilia*
referred to this clause of the Decemviral Code.
Hence it follows that the punishment provided by
this code was *nexum*, which is the view already
deduced from the words of the XII Tables themselves. The contrary interpretation, which is there-

---

[1] Festus, p. 376, *s.u. uindex*.   [2] VIII. 28.

fore probably erroneous, has strong supporters in Muirhead[1] and Voigt[2].

But even though a *iudicatum* was thus necessary in order to permit the nexal creditor to lead off his debtor into custody, we may agree with Muirhead that the preliminary *manus iniectio* was within the power of the nexal creditor without any judicial proceedings. The *nexum* being a public transaction, a debt thereby contracted was so notorious as to justify summary procedure. Before the XII Tables, when self-help was subject to no regulations that we can discover, this summary procedure could be carried to all lengths in the way of severity and cruelty. But when the XII Tables had interposed the *ductio in ius* for the protection of nexal debtors, no other precaution against injustice was needful, and a preliminary trial before the *manus iniectio* would have been so superfluous that we cannot believe it to have ever been required.

The elaborate provisions for the punishment of debtors did not end with the text which has come down to us and which has been quoted above. The substance, though not the actual wording, of the remainder of the law has fortunately been preserved by Gellius[3]. As far as our text goes, the proceedings consist of (1) *manus iniectio*, the arrest or seizure of the debtor by the creditor; (2) *ductio in ius*, the bringing of the debtor into court, that is, before the *praetor* or *consul*; (3) *iudicatum*, a decree of the *praetor* recognising the creditor's claim as just and the proceedings as

[1] *R. L.* p. 158.   [2] *XII Taf.* I. 629.   [3] xx. 1. 45–52.

properly taken. At this stage a *uindex* may step in on the debtor's behalf. What was the exact nature of his intervention we cannot know, but from Festus' definition he seems to have been a friend of the debtor, who denied the justice of his arrest and stood up in his defence. By the XII Tables he had to be of the same class as the debtor whom he defended[1], and if his assertions proved to be false he was liable to a heavy fine[2]. If on the other hand his defence was satisfactory to the Court, further proceedings were doubtless stayed. But if no satisfaction was given either by the *uindex* or by the debtor, then (4) the creditor was entitled to lead home his debtor in bondage, though not in slavery, and to bind him with cords or with shackles of not less than 15 lbs. weight. Meanwhile the law assumed that the debtor would prefer to live upon his own resources. This shows that a nexal debtor was not always a bankrupt, and that it must often have been the will and not the power to pay which was wanting in his case. As there existed in those days no means of attaching a man's property, the only alternative was to attach his person. If however the debtor was really a ruined man and could not afford to support himself, the law bade the creditor to feed him on the barest diet by giving him a pound of corn a day, or more at the creditor's option.

Here our textual information leaves off and we have to depend on Gellius' account. He says[3] that this stage of *domum ductio* and *uinctio* lasted sixty days, and that during that period a com-

[1] Gell. xvi. 10. 5.   [2] Festus, *s. u. uindex*.   [3] xx. 1. 46.

promise might be arranged which would stay further proceedings. Meanwhile (5) on three successive *nundinae*, or market-days, the debtor had to be brought into the *comitium* before the *praetor*, and there the amount of his debt was publicly proclaimed. This was a second precaution intended to protect the debtor by giving thorough publicity to the whole affair. At last (6) on the third market-day, and at the expiration of the sixty days, the full measure of punishment was meted out to the unfortunate delinquent: he was *addictus*[1] by the *praetor* to his creditor, and thus passed from temporary detention into permanent slavery.

The extreme penalty is said by Gellius to have been either death or foreign slavery, and the words in which the former was enacted are given by him as follows: TERTIIS NVNDINIS PARTIS SECANTO. SI PLVS MINVSVE SECVERVNT SE FRAVDE ESTO. The meaning of these words has been much disputed, for ever since the beginning of the century many attempts have been made to soften their literal sense. We should *a priori* translate them thus : " On the third market-day let the creditors cut up and divide the debtor's body. If any should cut more or less than his proper share, let him not suffer on that account." That this is how the ancients understood the passage, we know from the testimony of Gellius, Quintilian[2], and Tertullian[3]. But Gellius and Dio Cassius, though they had no doubts as to the meaning of the law, both say that

---

[1] Gell. xx. 1. 51.   [2] *Inst. or.* III. 6. 64.   [3] *Apol.* 4.

this barbarous practice of cutting a debtor in pieces
was never carried out, so far as they knew, even in
ancient times[1]. The law was therefore practically a
dead letter. Some commentators, whose views are
ably summed up by Muirhead[2], make the most
of this admission, and hold that the interpretation
of "*partis secanto*" should be entirely different.
They regard the division of the debtor's body
between the creditors as too shocking a practice
to have ever existed at Rome, and they take
secare to refer (as in the later phrase *bonorum sectio*)
to a sale and division of the debtor's property.
In the event of his property being insufficient
to cover the debt, the debtor would then, as
Gellius informs us, be sold into slavery "beyond
the Tiber." The objections to this theory have
been well pointed out by Niebuhr[3]. Not only is it
opposed to all the ancient authorities, who knew at
least the traditional meaning of the XII Tables as
handed down to them through many generations,
but it also conflicts with a well recognised principle
of early Law. That principle was that the goods of
a debtor were not responsible for his debts. His
person might be made to suffer, but his property
could not be touched. As we have seen, it was by
no means unusual for a nexal debtor to support
himself while in bondage. This can only be explained on the supposition that neither his property
nor his earnings were attachable by the creditor.
It is this exemption of property which accounts for

[1] Gell. xx. 1. 52. Dio Cass. *fragm.* 17. 8.
[2] *R. Law*, p. 208—9. [3] *R. G.* I. 630.

the severity of the nexal penalties. Now a sale and partition of the debtor's goods would have been quite inconsistent with the whole system of personal execution so plainly set before us in the rest of the law, whereas the killing of the debtor was but a fitting climax to his cruel fate. The inhumanity of the proceeding is not likely to have been perceived by men who tolerated such barbarities as the *lex talionis* and the killing of a son by his *paterfamilias*. When our classical authorities express their astonishment at the cruelty of the law, we must remember that they lived in a gentler age, in which the powers even of the *paterfamilias* were much curtailed; and when they confess that they never knew of an instance in which the law was literally executed, we may discount their testimony by recollecting that the nexal penalties of the XII Tables were abolished centuries before they wrote.

Comparative jurisprudence furnishes another argument in favour of accepting the literal sense of the phrase "*partis secanto.*" Kohler[1] has collected from different quarters various instances of customs which closely correspond with this harsh treatment of the Roman debtor. Unless therefore we disregard analogy, probability, and the whole of the classical evidence, we must clearly take the words literally and understand that the creditor could choose between selling his debtor into slavery "beyond the Tiber," or putting him to death. In the latter case, if there were more than one

[1] *Shakesp. v. dem Forum der Jurisp.*

creditor, they might cut up the body and each carry off a piece.

III. There is a third clause of the XII Tables in which *nexum* is mentioned, but it does not alter the form of the contract. As far as we can make out, it simply declares that certain persons mysteriously described as *forcti et sanates* shall have an equal right to the advantages of *nexum*[1].

IV. Lastly there is a clause of the XII Tables intended to secure truthful testimony, that most essential safeguard to *nexum*: QUI SE SIERIT TESTARIER LIBRIPENSVE FVERIT NI TESTIMONIVM FATIATVR IMPROBVS INTESTABILISQVE ESTO. That is, whoever had been *testis* or *libripens* at the performance of a *nexum* or *mancipium* was bound to give his testimony as to the fact of the transaction or as to its terms under penalty of permanent disqualification. This passage goes to show what we also gather from other authorities[2], that the *libripens* was a mere witness and not as some have supposed a public official. The phrase "*qui libripens fuerit*" would imply that any citizen might fill the position; and since we find that the *libripens* was treated like any other witness it seems clear that he could not have been a public personage.

We are now able to understand the meaning of Varro's remark: "*liber qui suas operas in seruitutem pro pecunia quam debet dat dum solueret nexus uocatur.*" This merely means that a man who had contracted a *nexum*, if unable to repay the

---

[1] See Festus *s. u. sanates*, Bruns *Font.* p. 364.

[2] Gai. II. 107 ; Ulp. *Reg.* xx. 7.

loan and therefore subject to an *addictio,* was obliged to serve like a slave, and retained the epithet of *nexus* till the debt was paid.

On the whole then the legislation of the XII Tables produced two results :

(1) By increasing the importance of the verbal part of the ceremony it increased the flexibility of the contract, and eventually changed it from a real into a symbolical transaction. The culminating point of the change was reached when the money constituting the loan was not weighed out, but merely named in the *nuncupatio,* while the borrower struck the scale-pan with a piece of copper.

(2) By fixing certain limits to the violence of the creditor it softened the hardships endured by the nexal debtor. Though the extreme penalty of death was finally permitted, yet this could not be inflicted till the debtor had had many opportunities and ample time to clear himself.

The formula of *nexum* having now acquired great importance, its wording was doubtless soon reduced to a definite shape running somewhat as follows : " *Quod ego tibi M libras hoc aere aeneaque libra dedi, eas tu mihi...post annum...cum semissario foenore...dare damnas esto.*" This is the formula adopted by Huschke[1] and modified by Rudorff. The words " *damnas esto* " appear to be wrongly rejected by Voigt, who disregards the analogy of the *solutio* though that seems our safest guide.

The formula of *nexi solutio* is given by Gaius[2] as follows, though Karlowa's reading differs consider-

<hr>

[1] *Nexum*, p. 49, etc.   [2] III. 174.

ably from that of Huschke : " *Quod ego tibi tot millibus condemnatus sum, me eo nomine a te soluo liberoque hoc aere aeneaque libra : hanc tibi libram primam postremamque expendo secundum legem publicam.*"

Art. 3. The XII Tables did not, as far as we know, contain any clauses affecting *sponsio* or *dotis dictio.* The existence of those forms at such an early period has to be inferred from other sources, and we have seen that there is reason to assert their great antiquity, which the silence of the XII Tables cannot disprove. *Iusiurandum* is known to have been approved by the XII Tables[1], but to what extent we cannot tell. We may therefore at once proceed to examine one of the most important innovations of the decemviral Code, namely the contract which despite its ambiguous name is known as the *lex mancipi.*

Art. 4. LEX MANCIPI. This form, as its name indicates, was a covenant annexed to the transaction known as *mancipium* (later as *mancipatio*). Let us see first what *mancipium* was. Ulpian[2] says that it was the mode of transferring property in *res mancipi.* Gaius describes its use shortly as a fictitious sale[3], " *imaginaria uenditio,*" and states that it could only be performed between Roman citizens, and applied only to *res mancipi*[4]. He describes the ceremony thus :—The parties meet in the presence of five witnesses and of a person (called *libripens*), who holds a pair of scales. The

---

[1] Cic. *Off.* III. 31 and see above, p. 39. [2] *Reg.* XIX. 3.
[3] I. 113. [4] I. 119–20.

object of the transfer Gaius supposes to be a
slave. The alienor remains passive, but the alienee,
grasping the slave, solemnly declares aloud that
he owns him by right of purchase; then he strikes
the scales with a piece of copper, and hands the
piece to the alienor as a symbol of the price paid.
Such is our meagre evidence as to the nature
of *mancipium*. On this slender foundation of fact
a vast amount of controversial theory has been
heaped up. One certainty alone can be deduced
from the evidence, that *mancipium* was not originally a general mode of conveyance, as Gaius and
Ulpian found it in their day, but that it began
by being a genuine sale for cash, in which the price
paid by the alienee was weighed in the scales and
handed over to the alienor. The *nuncupatio*, or
declaration made by the alienee, was merely explana-
tory of his right of ownership, while the grasping of
the object by the alienee and the acceptance of the
price by the alienor were no doubt originally the
essential elements in the transfer. The words spoken
by the alienee probably had at first no more binding
effect than the words of the borrower in *nexum*. We
may be sure that in such a state of the law disputes
would often arise as to the terms of the sale. And
it was probably to prevent such disputes that the
XII Tables made their famous rule: CVM NEXVM
FACIET MANCIPIVMQVE VTI LINGVA NVNCVPASSIT ITA
IVS ESTO. The extraordinary emphasis (not *nuncupassit* but *lingua nuncupassit*) which is here laid on
the verbal part of the ceremony is very striking.
Bechmann rightly argues that it would be wrong to

take this rule as referring only to the *leges mancipi*,
but it would seem that it was to the language as
distinct from the acts used in the ceremony that
the XII Tables meant to give force and validity.
The legal results which followed from seizing the
object of sale in the presence of witnesses, and
from weighing out the price to the seller, had
long since been thoroughly well recognised. What
the XII Tables now introduced was the recognition of the oral statement which accompanied
those outward acts. We can hardly accept the
sense which Bechmann has given to these words[1].
He notes the contrast between words and acts which
is implied in the phrase *lingua nuncupassit*, but he
thinks that the object of the rule was to reconcile
the language of the transaction with its real nature.
His view is based on the assumption that even
before the XII Tables *mancipium* had changed from
a genuine into a fictitious sale. In other words
he assumes that while the alienee professed to buy
the object with money weighed in the scales, he
really weighed no money, but simply handed to the
alienor a piece of copper, "*quasi pretii loco.*" In
fact the *imaginaria uenditio* of classical times was,
according to Bechmann[2], already in vogue. The
purpose of the XII Tables was therefore to confirm
this change, by declaring that the words and not the
acts of the parties should henceforth have legal
effect. It was as if this law said: "Pay no attention
to the acts of the alienee, but listen to his oral
statement. He merely delivers a piece of copper,

---

[1] *Kauf*, I. p. 197.   [2] *ib.* p. 167.

but do not imagine that this is the whole price due. In his declaration, the alienee states that the price is such and such. Let that be considered the real price of the object, and let the outward ceremony be regarded as a mere fiction." All this appears to be a very far-fetched interpretation of *lingua nuncupassit*, and the assumption on which Bechmann has based it seems unwarranted, for two reasons:

(1) We do not know that *mancipium* had already turned into an *imaginaria uenditio*. There is not one shred of evidence to prove that such a change had occurred before the XII Tables. So far indeed from preceding the XII Tables, the change would seem to have been directly caused by them. Until coin was introduced the weighing of the purchase-money was clearly necessary. If, as there is good reason to believe, coinage was first instituted by the Decemvirs[1], the actual weighing must have continued till their time. If on the other hand we suppose that coined money was a much older institution (Cornelius Nepos *de uir. ill.* 7. 8. attributes its invention to Seruius Tullius), so that the actual weighing had long been dispensed with, *mancipium* could still not have been an *imaginaria uenditio*, because

(2) We can imagine no way in which a sale on credit could have been practised before the XII Tables. How could a vendor have permitted his property to be conveyed to a purchaser for a nominal and fictitious price, when the *nuncupatio* was as yet devoid of legal force? After the *uti lingua nuncu-*

[1] See above, p. 42.

passit of the XII Tables the *nuncupatio* doubtless specified the exact amount of the purchase-money, and this the alienor might lawfully claim. Moreover before the Decemviral reforms *mancipium* would have transferred full ownership to the purchaser, and the seller might have clamoured in vain for his money, unless he had previously taken security by means of *uadimonium* or *sponsio*. For since a well known provision of the XII Tables[1] was that no property should pass in things sold till the purchase-money was either paid or secured, we are bound to infer that before this the very reverse was the case, and that property did pass even when the price had not been paid. Such having been the early law, how can we hold, as Bechmann does[2], that the cash payment of the purchase-money was frequently not required, though the forms of weighing etc. were carried out in the original manner? He urges[3] that credit, not cash, must often have been employed, because we cannot reasonably suppose that cash payment was possible in every case. But the force of this argument is weakened by the fact that mancipation was only practised to a limited extent. Tradition was the most ordinary mode of transfer employed in every-day life. And in a solemn affair such as *mancipium*, where five witnesses and a scale-holder had to be summoned before anything could be done, it cannot have been a great hardship for the purchaser to be obliged to bring his purchase-money and weigh it on the spot. Instead of credit purchases having been usual before the XII Tables,

[1] 2 *Inst.* 1. 41.   [2] *Kauf*, I. p. 160.   [3] *ib.* p. 158.

it seems likely that the XII Tables virtually introduced them. For by enacting that no property should pass until the price was paid or secured to the vendor, the Decemvirs made it possible for the conveyance and the payment of the price to be separately performed. *Mancipium* was thus made to resemble in one respect a modern deed. The vendor who has executed a deed, before receiving the purchase-money, has a vendor's lien upon the property for the amount of the price still owing to him ; and similarly the *mancipio dans* who had not received the full price, retained his ownership of the property until that full price was paid to him, or security given for its payment.

We may therefore reject Bechmann's idea that the words *lingua nuncupassit* referred principally to the fixing of price in the *nuncupatio*. They simply gave legal force to the solemn oral statement made in the course of *mancipium*. On the one hand they bound the seller to abide by the price named, and to deliver the object of sale in the condition specified by the buyer. On the other hand they compelled the buyer to pay the full price stated in the *nuncupatio*, and to carry out all such terms of the sale as were therein expressed. In short, every *lex mancipi* embodied in the *nuncupatio* became henceforth a binding contract.

It is natural to inquire next what kind of agreement might constitute a *lex mancipi*. The *nuncupatio* placed by Gaius[1] in the mouth of the purchaser runs thus : "*Hunc ego hominem ex iure*

---

[1] I. 119.

Quiritium meum esse aio, isque mihi emtus esto hoc aere aeneaque libra." To this might no doubt be annexed various qualifications, and these were the *leges* in question. Voigt[1] indeed considers that these *leges* might contain every conceivable provision, but Bechmann seems to come nearer to the truth in stating that no provision conflicting with the original conception of *mancipium* as a sale for cash could be inserted in the *nuncupatio.* For instance, Papinian states that no suspensive condition could be introduced into the formula of *mancipium*[2]. The reason of this obviously was that suspensive conditions are inconsistent with the notion of a cash sale. The purchaser could not take the object as his own and then qualify this proceeding by a condition rendering the ownership doubtful. A resolutive condition was also out of the question, for when the *mancipium* had transferred the ownership and the price was paid, it would have been absurd to say that the occurrence of some future event would rescind the sale. The transfer was in theory instantaneous, so that future events could not affect it.

The following then are a few cases in which the *lex mancipi* could or could not be properly used :

(*a*)   The creation of an usufruct by reservation could be thus made[3], and the formula is given to us by Paulus: *" Emtus mihi esto pretio deducto usufructu*[4]*."*

(*b*)   Property could thereby be warranted free

---

[1] *XII Taf.* II. 469.   [2] *Vat. Frag.* 329.
[3] *Vat. Frag.* 47.   [4] *Vat. Frag.* 50.

from all servitudes by the addition to the *nuncupatio* of the words "*uti optimus maximusque sit*[1]." The means by which the vendor was punished if the property failed to reach this standard of excellence will be presently examined.

(c) The contents and description of landed property might be inserted in the *nuncupatio*, and if they were so inserted the vendor was bound to furnish as much as was agreed upon. Failing this, the deceived purchaser, so Paulus tells us[2], could bring against the vendor an *actio de modo agri*, which entailed damages *in duplum*.

(d) The accessories of the thing sold, destined to be passed by the same conveyance, would also doubtless be mentioned.

(e) We might naturally have supposed that the quality of slaves or of cattle could have been described just as well as the content of an estate. Cicero says: "*cum ex XII Tabulis satis erat ea praestari quae essent lingua nuncupata*[3]," as though descriptions of all kinds might be given in the *nuncupatio*. Nevertheless Bechmann[4] has shown that such was not the case, inasmuch as we find no traces of any action grounded upon a false description of quality. The only actions which we find to protect *mancipium* are the *actio auctoritatis* and the *actio de modo agri*. There is no authority for supposing, as Voigt does[5], that the *actio de modo agri* was not a technical but a loose term used by Paulus. According to Voigt, there was an action

[1] 18 *Dig.* 1. 59. [2] *Sent.* I. 19. 1. [3] *Off.* III. 16. 65.
[4] *Kauf*, I. p. 249. [5] *XII Taf.* 120.

(the name of which has perished) to enforce all the terms of a *nuncupatio* of whatever kind. The so-called *actio de modo agri* would then have been only a variety of this general action. This theory is inadmissible: for in making his solemn list of the *actiones in duplum*[1], Paulus would hardly have used the clumsy phrase *actio de modo agri*, if there had been a comprehensive term including that very thing. Consequently, the description of slaves or cattle in the *nuncupatio* does not seem to have been in practice allowed. The greater protection thus afforded to a purchaser of land than to one of other *res mancipi* may probably be explained by the fact that land was not and could not be conveyed *inter praesentes*, whereas oxen or slaves could be brought to the scene of the *mancipium* and their purchaser could see exactly what he was buying.

(*f*) Provisions as to credit and payment by instalment might also be embodied as *leges* in the *nuncupatio*. This has been denied by Bechmann[2], Keller[3], and Ihering[4], but their reasons seem far from convincing. We may indeed fully admit their view for the period prior to the XII Tables, since there was then no coinage, and *mancipium* was an absolute conveyance of ownership. But when coinage had been introduced, when *mancipium* was capable of transferring *dominium* only after payment of the price, and when the oral part of *mancipium* had received legal validity from the XII Tables, the whole situation was changed.

---

[1] *Sent.* i. 19. 1.   [2] *Kauf*, i. p. 42.   [3] *Inst.* 33.
[4] *Geist d. R. R.*, ii. 530.

If it be said that credit is inconsistent with the notion of *mancipium* as an unconditional cash transaction, we may reply that this exceptional *lex* was clearly authorised by the XII Tables, since its use is implied in the legislative change above mentioned[1]. If it be urged that no action can be found to enforce any such *lex*, the obvious answer is that no action was needed, inasmuch as the ownership did not vest in the vendee till the vendor's claims were satisfied, and therefore if the vendee never paid at all the vendor's simple remedy was to recover his property by a *rei uindicatio*. Nor is there much force in the argument that clauses providing for credit would have been out of place in the *nuncupatio* because inconsistent with the formula "*Hanc rem meam esse aio, mihique emta esto.*" On the one hand it is probably a mistake to suppose that this fixed form was always used, for the expression *uti lingua nuncupassit* seems clearly to imply that the oral part of *mancipium* and *nexum* was to be framed so as best to express the intentions of the parties, and the same conclusion may be drawn from the comparison of the formulae of *mancipatio* given in Gaius[2]. On the other hand, admitting that "*hanc rem meam esse aio, etc.*" was a necessary part of the *nuncupatio*, it must have been used in mancipations made on credit, which by the XII Tables could not convey immediate ownership, and the existence of which in classical times no one denies. We are forced then to conclude either that "*hanc rem meam esse aio*" was not the phrase used at a sale on credit, or else

[1] 2 *Inst.* I. 41 and see p. 58.   [2] I. 119 and II. 104.

that it became so far a stereotyped form of words that it could be used not only in its literal sense but also as applying to credit transactions which the Decemviral Code so clearly contemplated. It is indeed inconceivable that if the price was, as every one admits, specified in the *nuncupatio,* the terms of payment should not have been specified also.

It is worth while to notice how the legal conception of *mancipium* was indirectly altered by the XII Tables. That very important clause which prevented the transfer of ownership in things sold, until a full equivalent was furnished by the vendee[1], had the effect of separating the two elements of which *mancipium* consisted. Delivery of the wares and receipt of the price had at first been simultaneous; they now could be effected singly. Thus *mancipium* became a mere conveyance, and after a while, as was natural, the notion of sale almost completely disappeared, so that *mancipium* came to be what it was in Gaius' system, the universal mode of alienating *res mancipi.*

The *lex mancipi,* as we have now considered it, was an integral part of the formula of *mancipium* which the vendee or alienee solemnly uttered. Gaius and Ulpian give us no hint that the vendor or alienor played any part beyond receiving the price from the other party. But was this really so? Could the vendee have known how to word his formula if the vendor had remained altogether silent? We have therefore to enquire next (1) what share the vendor took in framing the

[1] 2 *Inst.* 1. 41.

leges mancipi, and (2) how the *lex mancipi* was enforced against him.

1. The part played by the vendor is denoted in many passages of the Digest[1] by the word *dicere*. In others the word *praedicere*[2] or *commemorare*[3] expresses the same idea, and we find that the vendor sometimes made a written and sealed declaration[4]. The object of such *dicta* was to describe the property about to be sold[5], and they necessarily preceded the *mancipium*, or actual conveyance. They were thus no part of the mancipatory ceremonial and were quite distinct from the *nuncupatio* uttered by the vendee, which explains their not being mentioned by Gaius in his account of *mancipatio*[6]. It is to such *dicta* that Cicero doubtless alludes[7], when he says that by the XII Tables the vendor was bound to furnish only " *quae essent lingua nuncupata*," but that in course of time " *a iureconsultis etiam reticentiae poena est constituta.*" The *reticentia* here mentioned was evidently not that of the vendee, but was a concealment by the vendor of some defect in the object which he wished to sell, and hence this passage is useful as showing the contrast between *nuncupatio* and *dictum*. The former might repeat the statements contained in the latter, thus turning them into true *leges mancipi*, and this explains the fact that *lex mancipi* (or in the Digest *lex uenditionis*[8]), is sometimes used in the secondary

---

[1] e.g. 21 *Dig*. 1. 33, and 18 *Dig*. 1. 59.
[2] 19 *Dig*. 1. 21. fr. 1.   [3] 19 *Dig*. 1. 41.   [4] 19 *Dig*. 1. 13. fr. 6.
[5] 19 *Dig*. 1. 6. fr. 4.   [6] I. 119.
[7] *Off*. III. 16.   [8] 19 *Dig*. 1. 17. fr. 6.

sense of the vendor's *dictum*, as well as with the
primary meaning of the vendee's *nuncupatio*. The
leges embodied in the *nuncupatio* were thus binding
on the vendor, whereas his *dictum* was at first of no
legal importance. But in course of time the *dicta*
came also to be regulated, and though their terms
were not formal and were never required to be
identical with those of the *nuncupatio*, yet it was
essential that the vendor in making them should
not conceal any serious defects in the property. The
dictum itself produced no obligation ; that could only
be created by incorporating the *dictum* into the *nuncupatio*. The only function of *dictum* seems to have
been to exempt the vendor from responsibility and
from all suspicion of fraud. This is well illustrated
by a case to which Cicero[1] refers, where Gratidianus
the vendor had failed to mention, "*nominatim dicere
in lege mancipi*" (here used in the secondary sense),
some defect in a house which he was selling, and
Cicero remarks that in his opinion Gratidianus was
bound to make up to the vendee any loss occasioned
by his silence. Bechmann[2] questions whether the
action brought against Gratidianus was the *actio
emti* or the *actio auctoritatis*. But from the way in
which Cicero speaks, it seems almost certain that he
had been trying to bring a new breach of *bona fides*
under the operation of the *actio emti*, and had not been
pleading in a case of *actio auctoritatis*, which would
scarcely have been open to such freedom of interpretation. We cannot therefore agree with Bechmann that *dicta* not embodied in the *nuncupatio*

[1] *Or.* i. 39. 178.   [2] *Kauf*, i. p. 257.

could be treated as *nuncupata* and made the ground
for an *actio auctoritatis*, though we know that in
later times they could be enforced by the *actio emti*.
The distinction between the formal *nuncupata* and
the informal *dicta* was never lost sight of, so far as
we can discover from any of our authorities, nor is
dictum ever said to have been actionable until long
after the *actio emti* was introduced. The matters
contained in the *dicta* of the vendor were descriptions : (i) of fixtures or of property passing with an
estate[1], (ii) of servitudes to which an estate was
subject[2], (iii) of servitudes enjoyed by the estate[3]. It
is noticeable that these are all mere statements of
fact and that they exactly agree with the definition
given by Ulpian[4], who expressly excludes from *dictum*
the idea of a binding promise. Thus the distinction
between *nuncupatio* and *dictio* may be briefly summarized as follows :

Nuncupatio belonged only to *mancipium*, whereas
dictio might appear in sales of *res nec mancipi* as well
as in mancipatory sales[5].

Nuncupatio was a solemn and binding formula;
dictio was formless and, until the introduction of the
actio emti, not binding.

Nuncupatio, as we have seen, did not touch
upon the quality of the thing sold, whereas *dictio*
might give, and eventually was bound to give, full
information on this point.

We must notice in conclusion what Bechmann

[1] 19 *Dig.* 1. 26.
[2] 21 *Dig.* 2. 69. fr. 5.
[3] Cic. *Or.* I. 39. 179.
[4] 21 *Dig.* 1. 19.
[5] 19 *Dig.* 1. 6.

has pointed out[1], that *lex*, besides meaning a condition embodied in a sale or mancipation, signified also a general statement of the terms of a sale or hire. This sense occurs in Varro[2], Vitruvius[3], Cicero[4], &c., and should be borne in mind, in order to avoid confusion and to understand such passages correctly.

2.   The methods by which the true *leges nuncupatae* could be enforced were two :

(*a*)   *Actio de modo agri.* Of this we only know that it aimed at recovering double damages from the vendor who had inserted in the *nuncupatio* false statements as to the acreage of the land conveyed[5].

(*b*)   *Actio auctoritatis* (so called by modern civilians[6]). This was an action to enforce *auctoritas,* an obligation created by the XII Tables[7], whereby the vendor who had executed a mancipatory conveyance was bound to support the vendee against all persons evicting him or claiming a paramount title. *Auctor* apparently means one who supplies the want of legal power in another, and thereby assists him to maintain his rights. It is so used in *tutela,* of the guardian who gives *auctoritas* to the legal acts of his ward. In the present case, *auctor* means one who makes good another man's claim of title by defending it ; and this explains why the obligation of *auctoritas* varied in duration according to the nature of the thing sold. Thus if the thing was a moveable (e.g. an ox) the *auctoritas* of the vendor lasted only one year, since the *usucapio* of the vendee made it un-

---

[1] *Kauf*, i. p. 265.   [2] *L. L.* vi. 74.   [3] i. 1. 10.
[4] *Part. or.* 31. 107.   [5] Lenel, *Z. d. Sav. Stift.* R. A. iii. 190.
[6] Lenel, *Ed. perp.* p. 424.   [7] Cic. *Caec.* 19. 54.

necessary after that time. But if the thing sold was land, *usucapio* could not, by the XII Tables, take place in less than two years, and the *auctoritas* was prolonged accordingly[1]. The penalty for an unsuccessful assertion of *auctoritas* was a sum equal to twice the price paid[2]. This shows that at the date of the XII Tables, as we have seen, *mancipium* was still a genuine sale and involved the payment of the full cash price. The same conclusion may be drawn from Paulus' express statement that unless the purchase money had been received no *auctoritas* was incurred. This last rule was a logical sequence of the enactment that no property vested until payment was fully made, since it was impossible that the vendee should need the protection of an *auctor* before he had himself acquired title.

The question has been much debated whether this liability of a vendor to defend his purchaser's title arose *ipso iure* out of the mancipation, or whether it was the product of a special agreement. The latter view is held by Karlowa[3], and Ihering[4], but the weight of evidence against it seems to be overwhelming[5].

(*a*) Paulus[6] expressly states that warranty of title was given in sales of *res nec mancipi* by the *stipulatio duplae,* but existed *ipso iure* in sales by mancipation.

(*b*) Varro[7] says that if a slave is not conveyed

---

[1] Cic. *Top.* 4. 23.   [2] Paul. *Sent.* II. 17. 2–3.
[3] *L. A.* 75.   [4] *Geist des R. R.* III. 540.
[5] See Girard, in *N. R. H. de D.* 1882.   (6me Année) p. 180.
[6] *Sent.* II. 17. 1–3.   [7] *R. R.* II. 10. 5.

by mancipation, his purchaser's title should be protected by means of a *stipulatio simplae uel duplae*, thus implying that in cases of mancipation such a step was unnecessary.

(*c*) In recommending forms for contracts of sale, Varro advises the use of the *stipulatio* in sales of *res nec mancipi*[1], but gives no such advice and mentions no stipulatory warranty in the case of *res mancipi*.

(*d*) We find that there were two ways in which the vendor could escape the liability of *auctoritas*; either (i) he could refuse to mancipate[2], or (ii) he could have a merely nominal price inserted in the *nuncupatio* (the real price being a matter of private understanding between him and the vendee), so that the penalty for failing to appear as *auctor* would be a negligible quantity. This we actually find in a *mancipatio HS nummo uno*, of which an inscription has preserved the terms[3] where the object in mentioning so small a sum must have been to minimise the *poena dupli* in case the purchaser was evicted. Both these expedients to avoid liability are absolutely fatal to the theory of a special *nuncupatio* as the source of *auctoritas*. In short from all this evidence we must conclude that after the enactment of the XII Tables *mancipium* contained an implied warranty of the vendee's title.

The origin of the heavy penalty for failing to uphold successfully a purchaser's title has also been much debated. Bechmann[4] attributes its severity to

---

[1] *R. R.* II. 2. 6, and 3. 8.

[2] Plaut. *Pers.* 4. 3. 57.

[3] Bruns, *Font.* 251.

[4] *Kauf*, I. p. 121.

a desire to punish the vendor who had suffered his vendee to say "*hanc rem meam esse aio,*" when he knew that such was not the case. But this would have been to punish the vendor for *reticentia,* which was not done till much later times, as we know from Cicero; and moreover as we cannot be sure that the phrase "*hanc rem meam esse aio*" was invariably used in *mancipium*[1], this view of Bechmann's comes too near to the theory of the nuncupative origin of *auctoritas,* not to mention the fact that it fails to explain why the penalty was *duplum* instead of *simplum.* The best theory is probably that of Ihering[2], who sees in the *poena dupli* a form of the penalty for *furtum nec manifestum.* It may be true, as Girard has pointed out[3], that the *actio auctoritatis* was not an *actio furti* in every respect. The sale of land to which the seller has no good title lacks the great characteristic of *furtum,* that of being committed *inuito domino,* since the real owner of the land may often be entirely ignorant of the transaction. Still it is plain that the conscious keeping and selling of what one knows to be another man's property is a kind of theft; and, in that primitive condition of the law, it may have been thought unnecessary to impose different penalties on the *bona fide* vendor whose trespass was unconscious, and on the vendor who was intentionally fraudulent. This *poena dupli* can hardly be explained as a *poena infitiationis,* for if such, would not Paulus have been sure to mention it among his other instances of the latter penalty[4]?

[1] See above, p. 63.

[2] *Geist des R. R.* III. 229.

[3] *loc. cit.* p. 216.

[4] Paul. *Sent.* I. 19. 1.

Auctoritas had to be supplied by the vendor whenever any third person, within the statutory period of one or two years, attacked the ownership of the vendee by a *rei uindicatio*, or by a *uindicatio libertatis causa* if the thing sold was a slave, or by any other assertion of paramount title. Bechmann seems to be right in holding that the warranty of title also extended to all real servitudes enjoyed by the property, and to any other *accessiones* which had been incorporated in the *nuncupatio*. To attack the vendee's claim in that respect was to attack a part of the *res mancipata*. Hence *actio auctoritatis* was the remedy mentioned above[1] in connection with the true *leges mancipi*, and we may hold with Bechmann and Girard[2] that the *actio auctoritatis* and the *actio de modo agri* were the only available methods of punishment for the non-fulfilment of a *lex mancipi*.

How the vendor was brought into court as *auctor* is a question not easy to answer. But in Cicero[3] we find an action described as being *in auctorem praesentem*, and apparently opening with the formula: "*Quando in iure te conspicio, quaero anne fias auctor.*" The opening words do not lead us to suppose that the vendor had been summoned, but rather that he had casually come into court. This formula was probably uttered by the judge[4], in every case of eviction, before the inauguration of the *actio auctoritatis*, in order to give the defendant an opportunity of answering and so of avoiding the charge.

[1] See above p. 61. [2] *loc. cit.* p. 203.
[3] *Caec.* 19. 54; *Mur.* 12. 26. [4] Lenel, *Ed. Perp.* p. 427.

If no answer was made to this question, the vendor was held to have defaulted, and the vendee might properly proceed to bring his *actio auctoritatis* for punitive damages. But supposing that the *auctor* duly appeared to defend his vendee, what were his duties? It is not probable that he took the place of the vendee as defendant, because the word *auctor* does not seem to imply this, and because the vendor having conveyed away all his rights had no longer any interest in the property. The most probable solution seems to be that which regards the *auctor* simply as an indispensable witness. In the XII Tables we know[1] what severe penalties were laid upon a witness who did not appear, as well as upon one who bore false testimony. Now an *auctor* who appeared but failed to prove his case was clearly a false witness, while one who failed to appear was an absconding witness. This was probably an additional reason for the severe punishment inflicted on the *auctor* by the XII Tables. Thus the ingenious supposition of Voigt[2], that the vendor cannot possibly have incurred so heavy a penalty by mere silent acquiescence in the *nuncupatio* of the vendee, and must therefore have made a *nuncupatio* of his own in which he repeated the words used by the vendee, seems to be purely gratuitous as well as wholly unsupported by evidence.

The last question to be considered is this: did *auctoritas* apply solely to the warranty of things alienated by *mancipium*, or did it also apply to things alienated by *in iure cessio*? An answer in

[1] See above p. 52.   [2] *XII Taf.* II. 120.

the broader sense is given by Huschke[1], who cites Gaius[2], as proving that *mancipatio* and *in iure cessio* had identical effects. But this is at best a loose statement of Gaius', and cannot prevail against the stronger evidence which goes to prove that *auctoritas* was a feature peculiar to *mancipium*. Bekker[3] points out that *in iure cessio* cannot have produced the obligation of *auctoritas*, because the *in iure cedens* took no part in the proceedings beyond making default, and could not therefore have made deceptive representations rendering him in any way responsible. *In iure cessio* must then have been from its very nature a conveyance without warranty, and Paulus confirms this inference by stating[4] that the three requisites of *auctoritas* were (i) *mancipatio*, (ii) payment of the price, (iii) delivery of the *res*.

We may then sum up the foregoing remarks by defining *lex mancipi* and *auctoritas* as follows:

Lex mancipi in its primary meaning, was a clause forming part of the *nuncupatio* spoken by the vendee in the course of *mancipium*, and constituting a binding contract. It might embody descriptions of quantity, specifications of servitudes whether active or passive, conditions as to payment, and any other provisions not conflicting with the original conception of *mancipium* as a cash sale.

In its secondary meaning, which we must carefully distinguish, it referred to the *dicta* made by the vendor.

---

[1] *Nexum*, p. 9.
[2] II. 22.
[3] *Akt.* I. p. 33, note 10.
[4] *Sent.* II. 17. 1–3.

Thirdly, we even find it applied to the terms of sale as a whole, including *nuncupatio, dicta,* and any other private agreement between the parties respecting the sale.

The two means of enforcing *lex mancipi* in the first sense were *actio de modo agri* and *actio auctoritatis.*

Auctoritas was an implied warranty of title introduced by the XII Tables into every mancipatory conveyance, subject to the condition precedent that the vendee must have received the goods and paid the price. If the vendee was evicted, his proper remedy was the *actio auctoritatis* (most probably an instance of *legis actio sacramento*[1]), the object of which was to recover punitive damages of double the amount of the price paid, and which could be brought against the vendor within two years, if the object sold was an immoveable, and within one year, if a moveable.

Since the *lex mancipi* is often credited with a still wider function, we are next brought to consider the agreement known as *fiducia.*

Art. 5.   FIDVCIA.   This agreement is thought by many scholars to have been a species of *lex mancipi,* and consequently a creation of the XII Tables. Among those who thus regard *fiducia* as an agreement contained in the *nuncupatio* are Huschke[2], Voigt[3], Rudorff[4] and Moyle[5]. The first writer of any weight who disputed the correctness of this view

---

[1] Girard, *l.c.* p. 207.   [2] *Nexum,* pp. 76, 117.
[3] *XII Taf.* II. 477.   [4] *Z. für RG.* XI. 52.
[5] App. 2 to his ed. of the *Inst.*

was Ihering[1], and he has now been followed by Bekker[2], Bechmann[3], and Degenkolb[4]. The view held by these writers would seem to be the only tenable one. They assert that *fiducia* never was a part of *mancipium*, but was simply an ancillary agreement tacked on to *mancipium* and couched in no specific form. The arguments against the former theory are :

(1) That *fiducia* might exist in cases of *in iure cessio* as well as in cases of *mancipium*. Now *in iure cessio* gave no opportunity for the introduction of nuncupative contract. How then could a *nuncupatio* containing a *fiducia* have been introduced among the formalities of the *uindicatio* ?

(2) We know that the *actio fiduciae* was *bonae fidei*, and *bonae fidei* actions were of comparatively late introduction ; how then is this fact to be reconciled with the theory which derives *fiducia* from the *nuncupatio* of the XII Tables ? Voigt[5] states that the *actio fiduciae* was but one form of the ordinary action on a *lex mancipi* (it must be remembered that he regards every *lex mancipi* as having been actionable), but he gives no explanation of the surprising fact that *fiducia* alone of all the species of *lex mancipi* should have been provided with an *actio bonae fidei*.

(3) If we admit, as we have done[6], that the only actions based upon *mancipium* are the *actio auctoritatis* and the *actio de modo agri*, how can the *actio fiduciae* be classed with either ?

[1] *Geist des R. R.* II. p. 556.
[2] *Akt.* I. 124.
[3] *Kauf*, I. p. 287.
[4] *Z. für RG.* IX. p. 171.
[5] *XII Taf.* II. p. 475.
[6] *supra*, p. 68.

(4) The strongest piece of evidence which we possess in favour of Ihering's theory has appeared since he wrote. It consists of a bronze tablet inscribed with the terms of a *pactum fiduciae*[1] which Degenkolb[2] has carefully criticised and which seems to be conclusive in favour of our view. It contains, not a copy of the words used in mancipation, but a report of the substance of a fiduciary transaction. The mancipation is said to have taken place first, *fidi fiduciae causa*, and then the terms of the *fiducia* are said to have been arranged in a *pactum conuentum* between the parties, Titius and Baianus. It is evident from the language of the tablet that this fiduciary compact was independent of the *mancipatio* and informally expressed, so that any attempt, such as those made by Huschke and Rudorff, to reconstruct the formula of *fiducia*, and to fit such a formula into the *nuncupatio* of *mancipium*, is necessarily futile. Voigt[3] has even taken pains to give us the language used in the *arbitrium* by which, according to him, *fiducia* was enforced. This bold restoration is a good instance of Voigt's method of supplementing history, but it cannot be said materially to advance our knowledge.

We are nowhere told that *fiducia* could not be applied to cases of *traditio*, and *a priori* there is no reason why this should not have been the case. Yet all our instances of its use connect it solely with *mancipatio* or *in iure cessio*[4], and all the

---

[1] Printed in *C. I. L.* No. 5042 and Bruns, *Font.* p. 251.

[2] *Z. für RG.* IX. pp. 117—179.   [3] *XII Taf.* II. p. 480.

[4] Isid. *Orig.* V. 25. 23 ; Gai. II. 59; Boeth. *ad Cic. Top.* IV. 10, 41.

modern authorities, except Muther[1], are agreed in
thus limiting its scope.   If indeed we could extend
fiducia to cases of *traditio*, it would be very hard to
see why there should not have been a *contractus
fiduciae* as well as a *contractus commodati, depositi* or
pignoris.   We know from Gaius[2] that *fiducia* was
often practised with exactly the same purpose as
pignus or *depositum*, and we may reasonably infer
that it was the presence of *mancipatio* or *in iure
cessio* which caused the transaction to be described,
not as *pignus* or *depositum*, but as *fiducia*.   If we
admit that *fiducia* was never connected with *traditio*,
we can readily see why it never became a distinct
contract.   Bechmann[3] points out that *in iure cessio*
or *mancipatio* was naturally regarded as the principal feature in such transactions as adoptions,
emancipations, *coemtiones*, etc.   The solemn transfer
of ownership was in all these cases so prominent,
that *fiducia* was always regarded as a mere *pactum
adiectum*.

If then we cannot admit *fiducia* to any higher
rank than that of a formless *pactum*, it follows that
the *actio fiduciae*, being *bonae fidei*, and therefore
most unlikely to have existed at the period of the
XII Tables, must have originated many years later
than *fiducia* itself, which as a modification of
mancipatio probably dated from remote antiquity.
This may serve as an excuse for discussing *fiducia* in
this place, although the XII Tables do not actually
mention it.   But it must have existed soon after
that legislation, since it was the only mode of accom-

[1] *Sequestration*, p. 337.   [2] II. 60.   [3] *Kauf*, I. p. 293.

plishing the emancipation of a *filiusfamilias* as based
upon the XII Tables.

The theory that *fiducia* originated long before
the *actio fiduciae* is corroborated by the account
which Gaius gives[1] of the peculiar form of *usucapio*
called *usureceptio*. This was the method by which
the former owner of property which had been man-
cipated or ceded by him subject to a *fiducia* could
recover his ownership by one year's uninterrupted
possession. It differed from ordinary *usucapio* only
in the fact that the trespass was deliberate, and that
immoveable as well as moveable things could be thus
reacquired in one year instead of in two. This
peculiarity as to the time involved may perhaps be
explained by supposing that the objects of *fiducia*
were originally persons and therefore *res mobiles,* or
else consisted of whole estates which, like *hereditates,*
would rank in the interpretation of the XII Tables as
ceterae res. Now if *fiducia* had been incorporated, as
some think, in the formula of *mancipium,* and had been
actionable by means of an *actio fiduciae* based on the
lex mancipi, could not the owner have recovered the
value of his property by bringing this action, instead
of having been forced to abide the tedious and doubtful
result of a whole year's possession ? The fact noted
by Gaius that where no money was paid no *usureceptio*
was necessary, simply follows from the well-known rule
that an *in iure cedens* as well as a *mancipio dans* did
not lose his *dominium* until the price had been fully
paid to him. We may therefore conclude that *mancipatio fiduciae causa* resembled in its effect any

[1] II. 59–60.

other *mancipatio*. If this be the case, then *fiducia*, as we have already said, must for many years have been an informal and non-actionable *pactum*, supported by *fides* and by nothing else. Bechmann holds that[1] the object of the fiduciary mancipation was expressed in the *nuncupatio* by the insertion of the words *fidi fiduciae causa*, but this is a minor point which it is impossible to determine with certainty.

Fiducia then may be briefly described as a formless *pactum adiectum*, annexed to *mancipatio* or *in iure cessio*, but not originally enforceable by action, and therefore having no claim at this early date to be considered as a contract.

Art. 6. VADIMONIVM is a contract which we know to have been mentioned and perhaps introduced by the XII Tables[2]. Gellius, however, speaks of the ancient *uades*[3] as having completely passed away in his time, so that in the opinion of Karlowa[4] we can scarcely hope to discover the original form of the institution. The most thorough inquiry into the question is that made by Voigt[5], who has treated the authorities and sources with the minutest care, but whose conclusions do not always seem to be well founded.

Let us first examine the essence of the transaction, a point as to which there is no doubt. *Vas* meant a surety, and *uadimonium* the contract by which the surety bound himself. Thus *uadem*

[1] *Kauf*, I. p. 294.   [2] Gell. XVI. 10. 8.
[3] *ibid.*   [4] *L. A.* p. 324.
[5] *Phil. Hist. Abhandl. der k. S. Ges. d. Wiss.* VIII. 299.

poscere[1] meant to require a surety, *uadem dare* to provide a surety[2], *uadem accipere* to take a man as surety for another man[3], and *uadari* either to give surety or to be a surety[4]. From the point of view of the principal (*uadimonium dans*) *uadimonium sistere* meant to appear in due course[5], *uadimonium deserere*, to make default, while *uadimonium differre* meant to postpone the obligation which the *uas* had undertaken. The penalty for nonperformance was the payment (*depensio*) by the *uas* of the sum promised by his principal, who however was bound to repay him[6]. There might be more than one *uas*, and Voigt is probably right in stating that the *subuas* was a surety for the performance of the obligation by the original *uas*[7].

There were two kinds of *uadimonium*, (i) that which secured the performance of some contract[8]; (ii) that which secured the appearance of the party in court, = bail[9]. Under the first of these heads Voigt places the *satisdatio secundum mancipium* which is found in the Baetic *Fiduciae Instrumentum* as well as in Cicero[10], but whether or not this *satisdatio* was given in the form of a *uadimonium* must remain undetermined; though, if it had been so given, we might perhaps have expected Cicero to use the technical phrase.

[1] Cic. *Rep.* II. 36. 61; Var. *L. L.* VI. 8. 74.
[2] Cic. *Fin.* II. 24. 79.   [3] Cic. *Brut.* I. 18. 3.
[4] Prisc. *Gram.* I. 820.   [5] Cic. *Quint.* 8. 29.
[6] Cic. *ad Brut.* I. 18. 3.; Plaut. *Rud.* 3. 4. 72.
[7] *l. c.* p. 307.   [8] Varro, *L. L.* VI. 7. 71.
[9] Cic. *Off.* IV. 10. 45.   [10] *ad Att.* V. 1. 2.

Next comes the question, in what form was
uadimonium originally made ?

The verbal nature of the primitive contract seems
to be proved by the passages that Voigt quotes[1],
while he also completely demolishes the old view
which regarded *uadimonium* as having always been
a kind of stipulation, and points out Varro's[2] express statement that *uas* and *sponsor* were not the
same thing. On the other hand it is plain that
uadimonium had come by Cicero's time to denote
a mere variety of the stipulation, a fact which may
be gathered from his language[3] and that of Varro[4],
as well as from the frequent use of *promittere* in
passages describing the contract. The later aspect
of *uadimonium* need not however detain us, and
we may occupy ourselves solely with its primitive
form.

(*a*) Leist seems to think that both *uadimonium* and *praediatura* were binding, like the
sponsio, in virtue of a sacred "word-pledge," or in
other words that " *Vas sum*," " *Praes sum*," had a
formal value analogous to that of " *Spondeo*." This
view he bases on the etymology of *uas, praes* and
their cognates in the Aryan languages, but an examination of Pott[5], Curtius[6] and Dernburg[7] serves
to show how entirely obscure that etymology is. If
we cannot be sure whether *uas* is derived from *fari,*

---

[1] Cic. *ad Qu. fr.* ii. 15. 3.; Ovid, *Am.* i. 12. 23: *uadimonia
garrula*; etc.

[2] *L. L.* vi. 7. 71.   [3] *Quint.* 7. 29.   [4] *loc. cit.*

[5] *Etymol. Forsch.* iv. p. 612.   [6] *Civ. Stud.* iv. 188.

[7] *Pfdr.* i. 27.

to speak, *uadere,* to go, or from an Indo-Germanic
root meaning to bind, it is clearly impossible to
build any theory on so insecure a foundation. Moreover, whatever the true etymology of *uas* may
ultimately be proved to be, we can find in the above
derivations no suggestion of a binding religious
significance such as we discover in *sponsio.*

(*b*) Voigt boldly assumes a knowledge of the
ancient ceremony, and assigns to the *uadimonium*
connected with the sale of a farm the following
formula : " *Illum fundum qua de re agitur tibi habere
recte licere, haec sic recte fieri, et si ita factum non
erit, tum x aeris tibi dare promitto.*" This is not
only purely imaginary, like many of Voigt's reconstructed formulae, but the unilateral form in which
it is expressed has no justification from historical
sources. The scope of *promittis? promitto* in a
stipulation is well established, but how can *promitto* in an unilateral declaration have had any
binding effect ? Voigt justifies his view by a comparison with *dotis dictio* and *iurata operarum promissio*[1], but in both of these there was, as we have
seen, a binding power behind the verbal declaration.
The word *promitto* alone could never have produced
the desired effect, unless we admit the principle laid
down by Voigt[2] that an unilateral promise was sufficient to create a binding obligation, which is merely
to beg the question. If indeed we take *promittere* in
its ordinary sense, we cannot doubt that *uadimonium*
in Cicero's time was contracted by *sponsio* or *stipu-*

[1] *loc. cit.* p. 315.   [2] *Ius Nat.* iii. 178.

latio, but on the other hand it is equally certain that the ancient *uadimonium*, whatever it was, disappeared soon after the *Lex Aebutia*.

The old form known to the Decemvirs cannot then be stated with the absolute certainty which Voigt seems to assume, but we may hazard one theory as to its nature which appears not improbable, or at least far less so than that of an unilateral *promissio*. Gaius[1] tells us that there were several ways of making *uadimonia*, and that one of them was the ancient method of *iusiurandum*. That this was an exceptional method is proved by our rarely finding it in use[2], and its adoption is almost inconceivable, except in the earliest times when the oath was fairly common as a mode of contract. We may be sure that the old *uadimonium* was embodied in some particular form of words, else it is hard to imagine how the penalty could have been specified. But if so, and if we exclude *sponsio*, as we are bound to do, what form of words could have had such binding force as an oath ? The rarity of this oath in Gellius' time may have induced him to state that it had quite disappeared[3], while Gaius may have mentioned it in order to make his list of *uadimonia* complete.

Further, on examining the remedies for a breach of *iusiurandum*[4], we find that self-help was resorted to, just as it was in cases of *nexum*. And when self-help began to be restrained by law, the natural

---

[1] IV. 185.   [2] *e.g.* 2 *Dig.* 8. 16.
[3] See above p. 32.   [4] See above p. 11.

substitute would have been *manus iniectio.* Now
there is good reason to believe that the early
uadimonium was enforced by the *legis actio per
manus iniectionem*[1], and as Karlowa rightly says[2], we
cannot imagine such a severe penalty to have been
entailed by an ordinary *sponsio. Iusiurandum,* on
the contrary, may easily have had this peculiarity,
since it is the only form of verbal contract which
we know to have been protected by means of self-
help.

Again, *manus iniectio* seems to have been employed
not only by the principal against the *uas,* but also
by the *uas* against the principal. When Gaius states
that *sponsores* were authorized by a *Lex Publilia*
to proceed by *manus iniectio* against a principal
on whose behalf they had spent money (*depensum*),
he seems to show that facts and circumstances
were sometimes recognized as a source of legal
obligation. But we are bound to reject this explanation, since no obligation *ex re* was recognized
until much later in the Roman jurisprudence. It
is far more likely that, as Muirhead suggests[3], the
Lex Publilia merely extended to *sponsores* the
remedy already available to *uades*; so that *sponsio*
became armed with the *manus iniectio* simply on
the analogy of its older brother *uadimonium.* The
theory here put forward as to the early form of
uadimonium must remain a pure conjecture in the
absence of positive evidence; but its connection
with *iusiurandum* is at least a possibility.

[1] Karlowa, *L. A.* p. 325 : Voigt, *XII Taf.* ii. 495.
[2] *L. A.* p. 324.   [3] *R. L.* p. 166.

This vexed question may then be summed up as follows :

(i) In the legal system of the XII Tables *uadimonium* was a contract of suretyship, possibly entered into by *iusiurandum,* and probably entailing *manus iniectio,* (*a*) if the surety (*uas*) failed to fulfil his obligation, or (*b*) if the principal (*uadimonium dans*) failed to refund to his surety any money expended on his behalf.

(ii) In later times *uadimonium* was clothed in the ordinary *sponsio* and its old form had completely disappeared.

Art. 7. There are a few other fragmentary provisions in the XII Tables, which relate to contracts and require a brief notice.

I. Paulus[1] speaks of an *actio in duplum* as given by the XII Tables *ex causa depositi.* This cannot have had any connection with the *actio depositi* of the Institutes and Digest, for the latter was an invention of the Prætor (*honoraria*), and therefore could not have appeared till towards the end of the Republic, while its usual penalty was *simplum,* not *duplum.* Voigt explains[2] this action of the XII Tables as an instance of *actio fiduciae* based upon a *fiducia cum amico.* But we cannot admit that *fiducia* at such an early period was actionable at all[3], and still less can we base on Voigt's assumption the further theory that every breach of *fiducia* must have had ·a penalty of *duplum* annexed to it. The conjecture made by

[1] *Sent.* II. 12. 11. [2] *XII Taf.* II. 4. 79.
[3] See above, page 78.

Ubbelohde[1] that the *actio ex causa depositi* of the XII Tables was an *actio de perfidia* seems still more rash than that of Voigt, and has deservedly met with but little favour.

There are two points to be noted in this statement of Paulus:

(i) He states that the action was *ex causa depositi*: he does not call it *actio depositi*.

(ii) He does not say how the *depositum* was made, but implies that it might be made by *traditio* as well as by *mancipatio*, which also goes against Voigt's theory.

It was an ancient rule[2] that if a man used the property of another in a manner of which that other did not approve, he was guilty of common theft, and was punishable in *duplum* like any other *fur nec manifestus*. It seems therefore quite reasonable to suppose that the XII Tables mentioned this kind of *furtum* as arising *ex causa depositi*. If so, the penalty of *duplum* mentioned by Paulus is no mystery. It was merely the ordinary penalty assigned to *furtum nec manifestum*, and *depositum* as a contract had nothing to do with it. Hence this *actio ex causa depositi* does not properly belong to our subject at all.

II. Gaius[3] says that by the *pignoris capio* of the XII Tables (*a*) the vendor of an animal to be used for sacrifice could recover its value if the purchaser refused to pay the price, and (*b*) a man who had let a beast of burden in order to raise money for a sacrifice could recover the amount of

[1] *Gesch. der ben. R. C.* p. 22.   [2] Gai. III. 196.   [3] IV. 28.

the hire. Hardly anything is known of the *legis actio per pignoris capionem*, but it was evidently some proceeding in the nature of a distress, through which the injured party could make good his claim by seizing the property of the delinquent. The only points in which this passage of Gaius is instructive are these. First, we are here shewn what were evidently exceptional instances of the legal liability of a man's property, as distinguished from his person, for his breaches of agreement. Secondly, we here have conclusive proof that the consensual contracts of sale and hire were unknown at the period of the XII Tables: these two special instances in which the contracts were first recognised were both of a religious nature, and the makers of the XII Tables do not seem to have dreamt that other kinds of sale or hire needed the least protection. Thus for many years to come the most ordinary agreements of every-day life, such as hire, sale or pledge, were completely formless, depended solely on the honesty of the men who made them, and were not therefore, properly speaking, contracts at all. The principle of the old Roman law that neither consent nor conduct could create an obligation *ex contractu*, but that every contract must be clothed in a solemn form, appears in the fullest force throughout the XII Tables.

CHAPTER IV.

THE DEVELOPMENT OF CONTRACT.

AT the threshold of a new period we may pause
to review briefly the ground already covered, and to
observe the very different aspect of our future field
of inquiry.

We find the legal system of the XII Tables to
have possessed five distinct forms of contract,
iusiurandum (including *uadimonium ?*), *sponsio, dotis
dictio, nexum,* and *lex mancipi.* But though the
list sounds imposing enough, these forms were still
primitive and subject to many serious limitations:

(i) Roman citizens only were capable of using
them, and hence they were useless for purposes of
foreign trade.

(ii) They all alike required the presence of
the contracting parties, and were therefore available
only to persons living in or near Rome.

(iii) They all required the use of certain formal
words or acts, so that, if the prescribed formula or
action was not strictly performed, the intended
contract was a nullity.

(iv) The remedies for a breach of contract,
except in the case of *nexum* and *lex mancipi,* were
probably of the vaguest description, and may have
consisted only of self-help carried out under certain
pontifical regulations.

A system with so many flaws was plainly incapable of meeting the many needs which grew out of immense conquests and rapidly extending trade. Accordingly by the end of the Republic we find that the law of contract had wholly freed itself from every one of these four defects :

(i) Contracts had been introduced in which aliens as well as Romans could take part.

(ii) Means had been devised for making contracts at a distance.

(iii) Forms had by degrees been relaxed or abolished.

(iv) Remedies had been introduced by which not only the old contracts but all the many new ones were made completely actionable.

The question now before us is : how had this wonderful development been achieved ?

It is customary in histories of Roman Law to subdivide the period from the XII Tables to the end of the Republic into two epochs, the one before the *Lex Aebutia*, the other subsequent to that law. The reason for this subdivision is that the *Lex Aebutia* is supposed to have abolished the *legis actio* procedure and to have introduced the so-called formulary system, which enabled the Praetors to create new forms of contract by promulgating in their Edict new forms of action.

Such a division doubtless has the merit of giving interest and definiteness to our history, but it has two great drawbacks : First, that we do not know what the *Lex Aebutia* did or did not abolish ; and secondly, that its date is impossible to determine.

As to its provisions, the two passages in which the law is mentioned by Gaius[1] and Gellius[2] merely prove that the *legis actio* system of procedure and various other ancient forms had become obsolete as a result of the *Lex Aebutia*. But that these were not suddenly abolished is proved by the well-known fact that Plautus and Cicero refer more often to the procedure by *legis actiones* than they do to that *per formulas*. The most plausible theory seems to be that which regards the *Lex Aebutia* as having merely authorized the Praetors and Aediles to publish new *formulae* in their annual Edicts. But even this is nothing more than a conjecture.

The date of the *Lex Aebutia* (probably later than A. V. C. 500) is also involved in obscurity, as is proved by the fact that scarcely two writers agree upon the question[3].

It seems clear that a law about which so little is known is no proper landmark. The plan here adopted will therefore be a different one. We shall content ourselves with a detailed examination of each of the kinds of contracts which we know to have existed at Rome between the XII Tables and the beginning of the Empire, treating in a separate section of each contract and its history down to the end of the period. By this means we may avoid confusion and repetition, though the period in hand, extending as it does over nearly five hundred years, is perhaps inconveniently large to be thus treated as a whole.

[1] IV. 30.　　　　　　　　[2] XVI. 10. 8.

[3] A. V. C. 584 according to Poste and Moyle; 513 according to Voigt; 507 according to Muirhead; etc.

CHAPTER V.

FORMAL CONTRACTS OF THE LATER REPUBLIC.

Art. 1. NEXVM. The severity and unpopularity of *nexum* did not prevent its continuance for at least one hundred years after the modifications made in it by the XII Tables. Its character remained unchanged, until at last the Roman people could suffer it no longer. In A. V. C. 428[1] a certain *nexus* was so badly treated by his creditor that a reform was loudly demanded. The *Lex Poetilia Papiria* was the outcome of this agitation. Cicero[2], Livy[3] and Varro[4] have each given a short account of the famous law, and from these it may be gathered that its chief provisions were as follows:

(i) That fetters should in future be used only upon criminals.

(ii) That all insolvent debtors in actual bondage who could swear that they had done their best to meet the claims of their creditors[5], should be set free.

---

[1] According to Livy, but Dionysius makes it 452.
[2] *Rep.* II. 30. 40. 59.   [3] VIII. 28.   [4] *L. L.* VII. 5. 101.
[5] *Nexi qui bonam copiam iurarent*: cf. *Lex Iul. Mun.* 113.

(iii) That no one should again be *nexus* for borrowed money, i.e. that *manus iniectio* and the other *ipso iure* consequences of *nexum* should henceforth cease.

Varro is the one writer who mentions the qualification that it was only *nexi qui bonam copiam iurarent* who were set free. But Cicero and Livy may well have thought this an unnecessary detail, considering what an immense improvement had been made by the statute in the condition of all future borrowers. A clause of the *Lex Coloniae Iuliae Genetiuae*[1] shows that imprisonment for debt was still permitted, but that the effects of *ductio* were much softened, the *uinctio neruo aut compedibus* and the capital punishment being abolished along with the *addictio*. But *duci iubere* was still within the power of the magistrate[2], and Karlowa[3] seems to be right in holding that this was not a new kind of *ductio* originating subsequently to the *Lex Poetilia.* The Praetor doubtless always had the power to order that a *iudicatus* should be taken and kept in bonds. But this was a very different thing from the utterly abject fate of the *nexus* under the XII Tables. It was only therefore the special severities consequent upon *nexum* that can have been abolished by the *Lex Poetilia. Nexum* itself was not abrogated, for the way in which later authors speak of it shows that there still survived, if only in theory, a form bearing that name and creating an obligation. But as soon as its summary remedies were taken

---

[1] cap. 61; Bruns, *Font.* p. 119.

[2] *Lex Rubr.* cap. 21 ; Bruns, *Font.* p. 98.   [3] *L. A.* p. 165.

away, *nexum* became less popular as a mode of contract and gave way to the more simple *obligatio uerbis*. Another reason for its being disused, when it no longer had the advantage of entailing capital punishment, was that the introduction and widespread use of coinage made the use of scales unnecessary. *Stipulatio*, which required no accessories and no witnesses, was now the easiest mode of contracting a money loan. We shall see in the next section that it came to have still further points of superiority, and thus it was certain to supersede *nexum*, when *nexum* ceased to have special terrors for the delinquent debtor.

The *solutio per aes et libram* which we find in Gaius, as a survival of *solutio nexi*, was not the release of *nexum*, but the similar release used for discharging a legacy *per damnationem* or a judgment debt. Its continued existence is no proof that *nexum* survived along with it, for in later days it had nothing to do with the release of borrowed money. But though *nexum* proper certainly died out before the Empire, we have seen[1] how the meaning of the word became more vague and comprehensive. By the end of the Republic we find *nexum* used to describe essentially different transactions, and simply denoting any *negotium per aes et libram*.

Art. 2. SPONSIO and STIPVLATIO. The origin and early history of *sponsio* have already been considered. There is no authority for Bekker's opinion that *sponsio* was enforceable before the XII Tables by the *legis*

[1] See above p. 24.

actio sacramento[1], nor do we know that it gave rise to any action, but notwithstanding this fact we have seen good reason for concluding that it existed at Rome from the earliest times. As we found that its origin was religious, and as the XII Tables do not mention it, we may regard the remedies for a breach of *sponsio* as having been regulated by pontifical law, down to the time when *condictiones* were introduced. In the law of this last period *sponsio* appears in three capacities:

(1) As a general form of contract adapted to every conceivable kind of transaction.

(2) As a form much used in the law of procedure.

(3) As a mode of contracting suretyship.

Its binding force was the same in all these three adaptations, but its history was in each case different. Thus *sponsio* was used as a general form of contract down to the time of Justinian, though it had then long since disappeared as a form of suretyship. And there were statutes affecting the *sponsio* of suretyship which had nothing to do with the *sponsio* of contract or of procedure. It will therefore be convenient to treat, under three distinct heads, of the three uses to which *sponsio* became adapted, remembering always that in form, though not in all its remedies, it was one and the same institution.

I. *Sponsio as a general form of contract.*

We have seen that the form of *sponsio* consisted of a question put by the promisee and answered by the promisor, each of whom had to use the

[1] *Akt.* i. p. 147.

word *spondere*. For example: Qu.: "*Sponden tuam gnatam filio uxorem meo?*" Ans.: "*Spondeo*[1]." Qu.: "*Centum dari spondes?*" Ans.: "*Spondeo*[2]." This form was available only to Roman citizens. But there subsequently came into existence a kindred form called *stipulatio*, which could be used by aliens also, and could be expressed in any terms whatsoever, provided the meaning was made clear and the question and answer corresponded.

The connection between *sponsio* and *stipulatio* is the first question which confronts us. There is no doubt that *sponsio* was the older form of the two, because (i) it alone required the use of the formal word *spondere*, (ii) it was strictly *iuris ciuilis*, whereas *stipulatio* was *iuris gentium*[3], and (iii) it had to be expressed in the present tense (e.g. *dari spondes?*) whereas *stipulatio* admitted of the future tense (e.g. *dabis? facies?*), which Ihering[4] has shown to be a sign of later date. Since the rise of the *ius gentium* was certainly subsequent to the XII Tables, we are justified in ascribing to the *stipulatio* a comparatively late origin, though the precise date cannot be fixed with certainty.

Though *stipulatio* was a younger and a simplified form, yet it is always treated by the classical jurists as practically identical with *sponsio*. Both were verbal contracts *ex interrogatione et responsione*, and their rules were so similar that it would have been waste of time and useless repetition to discuss them separately.

[1] Varro, *L. L.* vi. 7. 70.   [2] Gaius iii. 92.
[3] Gaius *loc. cit.*   [4] *Geist d. R. R.* ii. 634.

The derivation of *stipulatio* has been variously given. Isidorus[1] derived it from *stipula*, a straw; Paulus Diaconus[2] and Varro[3] from *stips*, a coin; and the jurist Paulus[4], followed by the Institutes, from *stipulus*, firm. The latter derivation is doubtless the correct one[5], but it does not help us much. What we wish to know is the process by which a certain form of words came to be binding, so that it was distinctively termed *stipulatio*, the firm transaction. Now if we conclude, as Voigt does[6], that the *stipulatio* and the *sponsio* were both imported from Latium, their marked difference with respect to name, age and form must remain a mystery. Whereas we may solve, or rather avoid, this difficulty by acknowledging that *sponsio* was the parent of *stipulatio*, and that the latter was but a further stage in the simplification of *sponsio* which had been steadily going on since the earliest times. We have already reviewed the three stages through which *sponsio* seems to have passed. *Stipulatio* in all probability represents a fourth and wider stage of development. The binding force of a promise by question and answer, apart from any religious form, at last came to be realized after centuries of use[7], and as soon as the promise became more conspicuous than the formal use of a sacred word, the word *spondere* was naturally dropped, and with

---

[1] *Orig.* 5. 24.
[2] *s. u. Stipem.*
[3] *L. L.* vi. 7. 69–72.
[4] *Sent.* v. 7. 1.
[5] See Ihering, *Geist* ii. § 46, note 747, who compares the German *Stab, Stift, bestätigen, beständig*.
[6] *Ius Nat.* ii. 238.
[7] Ihering, *Geist* ii. p. 585.

it fell away the once descriptive name *sponsio*, to make way for that of *stipulatio*, now a more correct term for the transaction. Thenceforward, as a matter of course, *stipulatio* became the generic name, while *sponsio* was used to denote only the special form *spondesne? spondeo*.

The precise date of the final change is a matter of guess-work. But as *stipulatio* was the form available to aliens[1], it was probably the influx of strangers which made the Romans perceive that their old word *spondere*, only available to Roman citizens, was inconvenient and superfluous. Unless contracts with aliens had become fairly common, the need of the untrammelled *stipulatio* would hardly have been felt. Therefore it seems no rash conjecture to suppose that the *stipulatio* was first used between Romans and aliens, and first introduced about A.V.C. 512[2], the date generally assigned to the creation of the new Praetor *qui inter peregrinos ius dicebat*.

As to the form of the *stipulatio*:

(*a*) Ihering[3] and Christiansen[4] have expressed the opinion that originally the promisor did not merely say *spondeo, faciam, dabo*, etc., as in most of the known instances, but repeated word for word all the terms of the promise as expressed in the question put by the promisee. This view is based upon the passages in Gaius[5] and the Digest[6], which lay great stress upon the minute correspondence necessary between the question and the answer in a valid

---

[1] Gai. III. 93.

[2] Liu. *Epit.* XIX.

[3] *Geist* II. 582.

[4] *Inst. des R. R.* p. 308.

[5] III. 92.

[6] 45 *Dig.* 1. 1.

stipulation. It is hard to see how such a rule could have arisen unless there had been some danger of a mistake in the promisor's reply, and if this reply had been confined to the one word *spondeo*, *promitto*, or *faciam*, a mistake would hardly have been possible. Hence this view seems highly probable.

(*b*) Voigt[1] has given the following account of the origin of the various formulae.

(i) The form *spondesne? spondeo* is the oldest of all, and dates back into very early times[2], which is probably quite correct. But in a more recent work[3] this view expressed in *"Ius Naturale"* is unfortunately abandoned, and Voigt regards *sponsio* as a Latin innovation dating from the fourth century of the City. This seems surely to place the birth of *sponsio* far too late in Roman history.

(ii) The looser form *dabisne? dabo* is found in Plautus[4], and was no doubt, as Voigt says[5], a product of the *ius gentium* and first introduced for the benefit of aliens.

(iii) Lastly, the origin of the forms *promittis? promitto*, and *facies? faciam*[6], is placed by Voigt not earlier than the beginning of the Empire. But his reasons for so doing seem most inadequate. If the form *dabisne? dabo* occurs in Plautus, the form *facies? faciam*, which is essentially the same, can hardly be attributed to a later period. And since

---

[1] *Ius Nat.* IV. 422 ff.
[2] See Liu. III. 24. 5, A.V.C. 295, and III. 56. 4, A.V.C. 305.
[3] *Röm. RG.* I. p. 43.   [4] *Pseud.* 1. 1. 112, A.V.C. 563.
[5] *I. N.* IV. 424.   [6] Cf. Gaius, III. 92. 116.

promittam is used by Cicero as a synonym for *spondeam*[1], and *fidepromittere* was an expression used in stipulations, as Voigt admits, two centuries before the end of the Republic[2], it seems rash to affirm that *promittere*, the shortened phrase, was not used in stipulations until the time of the Empire. We may therefore attribute both of these forms to republican times.

(c) The admissibility of *condicio* and *dies* as qualifications to a stipulation must always have been recognized, since a promise deals essentially with the future and requires to be defined.

(d) The insertion of a conventional penalty into the terms of the contract was probably practised from the very first, whenever *facere* and not *dare* was the purport of the promise, because the *condictio certi* was older than the *condictio incerti*, and therefore for many years an unliquidated claim would have been non-actionable unless this precaution had been taken.

We have now seen that verbal contract by question and answer, whether called *sponsio* or *stipulatio*, existed long before it became actionable. When it finally became so is uncertain, though we know what forms the action took.

(a) *Condictio certae pecuniae.*

Gaius[3] speaks of a *Lex Silia* as having introduced the *legis actio per condictionem* for the recovery of *certa pecunia credita*. This law is mentioned nowhere else, and its date can only be approximately fixed.

---

[1] Cic. *pro Mur.* 41. 90.   [2] *I. N.* IV. 424, note 77.
[3] IV. 19.

We know from Cicero[1] that *pecunia credita,* a regular money loan, might in his time originate in three ways, by *datio (mutuum), expensilatio,* or *stipulatio.* But we cannot infer from this that the *Lex Silia* made all those three forms of loan actionable[2], for *mutuum* and *expensilatio,* as will presently be seen, were certainly of more modern origin than the *condictio certae pecuniae.* It appears indeed that *stipulatio* was the original method of creating *pecunia credita*[3]: consequently the *Lex Silia* must have simply provided for the recovery of loans made by *sponsio* or *stipulatio.* It is noticeable, moreover, that Gaius speaks as though by this law money debts had merely been provided with a new action: he does not imply that *stipulatio* or *sponsio* was thereby introduced, as Voigt[4] and Muirhead[5] have ventured to infer. Their view is surely an unwarrantable inference, for if the *Lex Silia* had created so new and important a contract as *stipulatio,* Gaius would hardly have expressed so much surprise at the creation of a new form of action to protect that contract. His language seems clearly to imply that *pecunia credita* was already known, and was merely furnished by this law with a new remedy. We may conclude then that *pecunia credita* must have existed before the *Lex Silia,* and can only have been created by *stipulatio. Stipulatio*

---

[1] *Rosc. Com.* 5. 14.   [2] Puchta, *Inst.* 162.

[3] Cf. the *dare, credere, expensum ferre* of the *Instrumentum fiduciae* in Bruns, p. 251, with the *dare, stipulari,* and *expensum ferre* of *Rosc. Com.* 5. 13–14, and see Voigt, *Ius Nat.* iv. 402.

[4] *Ius Nat.* ii. 243.   [5] *R. L.* p. 230.

cannot, therefore, have been introduced by this law, though it probably was thereby transferred from the religious to the secular code.

The age of the *Lex Silia* has been variously given[1], but there are no trustworthy data, and any attempt to fix it must be somewhat conjectural. The only thing we do know is that this law must have been enacted a considerable time before the *Lex Aquilia* of A.V.C. 467, for the latter law punished[2] the *adstipulator* who had given a fraudulent release, and as this release must have applied to the *stipulatio certae rei* of the *Lex Calpurnia*[3], it is evident that the *Lex Aquilia* must have been younger than the *Lex Calpurnia*, which, as we shall see, was itself younger than the *Lex Silia*.

We may perhaps approximate even more closely to the date of the *Lex Silia*. Muirhead[4] has conjectured with much plausibility that the introduction of the *condictio certae pecuniae* was a result of the abolition of the nexal penalties, or in other words that the *Lex Silia* followed soon after the *Lex Poetilia* of A.V.C. 428. There are several strong points in favour of this hypothesis:

(i) It explains Gaius' difficulty as to the reason why *condictio* was introduced. For when the terrors of *nexum* were abolished, it was natural to substitute some penalty of a milder description and not to let defaulting debtors go entirely unpunished. Now

---

[1] A.V.C. 311 to 329, according to Voigt, *I. N.* IV. 401.

[2] Gai. III. 215.

[3] Cf. *quanti ea res est* in Gai. *loc. cit.* with 13 *Dig.* 3. 4.

[4] *R. L.* p. 230.

this is just what the *condictio certae pecuniae,* with its *sponsio poenalis tertiae partis,* presumably accomplished, for like *nexum* it dealt only with *pecunia.*

(ii) This hypothesis helps us also to understand why the *condictio certae pecuniae* should have been introduced before the *condictio certae rei,* thus making a stipulation of *certa pecunia* actionable, while a stipulation of *res certa* had not this protection. As we found above[1], the introduction of coin must have made the *stipulatio certae pecuniae* a very convenient substitute for *nexum.* It was therefore natural to give a remedy to this *stipulatio* and so to make it take the place of *nexum* as a binding contract of loan; while *certa res,* never having had and therefore not immediately requiring a remedy, was not protected by *condictio* until several years later.

(iii) We can also see why the *condictio certae pecuniae* should have been the only *condictio* furnished with so severe a penalty as the *sponsio poenalis.* It was because money loans had been jealously guarded in the days of *nexum,* and it was therefore thought proper to protect the money loan by stipulation far more carefully than the promise of a *res certa.*

All these seem strong points in confirmation of Muirhead's hypothesis. By connecting *stipulatio* and *condictio* with the downfall of *nexum* and of its *manus iniectio,* we not only get a plausible date for the *Lex Silia,* but what is far more important, we

[1] p. 94.

obtain a satisfactory explanation of the curious fact
that, while *stipulationes* were made actionable, they
were not all made so at once.

The forms of *condictio* under the *legis actio* system
are not known, but under the formulary system, this
condictio had the following formula: *Si paret N^m
Negidium A^o Agerio HS X dare oportere, iudex, N^m
Negidium A^o Agerio X condemna. s. n. p. a.*[1] Its
peculiar *sponsio* will be given in another place.

(*b*) *Condictio triticaria or certae rei.*

The *Lex Calpurnia*, which must have preceded
the *Lex Aquilia*[2] and must therefore have been
enacted earlier than A.V.C. 467, extended the *legis
actio per condictionem* to stipulations of *triticum*, corn,
(*condictio triticaria*); and this, being soon interpreted
by the jurists as including every debt of *res certa*,
gave rise to the *condictio certae rei*. This new kind
of *condictio* omitted, for the reason above[3]-stated, the
sponsio and *restipulatio tertiae partis*, in place of
which the defendant merely promised to the plaintiff
a *nummus unus* which was never exacted or paid[4].
Therefore, as the severer law invariably precedes the
milder, we might be sure that the *Lex Silia* with its
heavy penalty was older than the *Lex Calpurnia*
with its nominal fine[5], even if Gaius had not clearly
led us to this conclusion by the order in which he
mentions the two laws[6].

The formula ran thus: *Si paret N^m Negidium A^o
Agerio tritici optimi X modios dare oportere, quanti*

---

[1] Gai. IV. 41. Lenel, *Ed. Perp.* 187.   [2] See above, p. 102.

[3] p. 103.   [4] Voigt, *I. N.* III. 792.

[5] Keller, *Civilp.* 20.   [6] Gaius, IV. 19.

ea res est, tantam pecuniam, iudex, N^m Negidium A^o Agerio condemna. s. n. p. a.

(c)   *Condictio incerti.*

The above *condictio triticaria*, or *certae rei*, was in course of time extended by the interpretation of the jurists or by the Praetor's Edict to *res incertae*, and gave rise to a *condictio incerti*, which was the proper action on a stipulation involving *facere* or *praestare* or some other object of indefinite value. The thing promised might be defined as *quanti interest*, or *quanti ea lis aestimata erit* etc.[1], and it is plain how much this comprehensive mode of expression must have increased the adaptability and general usefulness of the stipulation. In this way, for instance, the *cautio damni infecti* and the stipulations of warranty were doubtless always expressed. The nature of this *condictio* may perhaps be best understood from its formula, which was as follows: *Quod A^s Agerius de N^o Negidio incertum stipulatus est, quidquid paret ob eam rem N^m Negidium A^o Agerio dare facere oportere, eius iudex, N^m Negidium A^o Agerio condemna. s. n. p. a.*[2] This was so far an advance upon the *condictio certae rei* that the *condemnatio* here left the damages entirely to the discretion of the judge; but it was still a *stricti iuris* action, in which no equitable pleas were admitted on the part of the defendant.

(d)   *Actio ex stipulatu.*

We have seen that the *condictiones certae pecuniae* and *certae rei* were due to legislation, and the *condictio incerti* to juristic interpretation: it remains

---

[1] Voigt, *RG.* I. pp. 601–2.   [2] Gai. IV. 131, 136.

to inquire what was the origin of the *actio ex stipulatu*, i.e. the *bonae fidei* action on a stipulation for *incertum dare* or for *certum facere*[1], which completed this series of legal remedies. Its appearance was an event of great importance to the subsequent history of Contract, since it applied exclusively to stipulations containing a *bonae fidei clausula*, and it was by means of this action alone that such stipulations were enforced[2]. Voigt's explanation of its origin is that the *actio ex stipulatu* was devised as the proper remedy for *fidepromissio* and for the *cautio rei uxoriae* introduced in A.V.C. 523[3]. But it is very doubtful if the date can be fixed with such exactness. There is nothing to show that the *actio ex stipulatu* did not exist earlier than those particular forms of stipulation; and if it had been, as Voigt thinks, the original action on a *fidepromissio*, it would probably have been known as *actio ex fidepromisso* or by some such descriptive name.

The introduction of the *doli clausula* is the most important event in the whole history of the *stipulatio*, yet the exact moment at which this took place is hard, if not impossible, to fix. Girard[4] attributes its invention to C. Aquilius Gallus. But if this had been the case, Cicero[5] would hardly have overlooked the fact. On the other hand Voigt, who rightly identifies the *actio ex stipulatu* with the action on a

---

[1] Bethmann-Hollweg, *C. P.* p. 267.

[2] 44 *Dig.* 4. 4. fr. 15–16.

[3] *I. N.* IV. 407. Gellius IV. 1, 2.

[4] *N. Rev. Hist. de Droit*, XIII. 93.   [5] *Off.* III. 14. 60.

doli clausula, and regards the two as inseparable, places the introduction of *doli clausula* earlier than the time of Cicero, because that writer mentions the *actio ex stipulatu* among the " *iudicia in quibus additur ' ex fide bona*[1].' " The introduction of the first *clausula doli* was, according to Voigt[2], made by the words *fides,* in *fidepromissio,* and "*quod melius aequius sit*" in the *cautio rei uxoriae*[3]. This conjecture is unsupported by evidence; for though we know that *cautio rei uxoriae*[4] and *fidepromissio*[5] were both actionable by the *actio ex stipulatu,* and therefore must have contained *doli clausulae,* we have no right to assume that they were the first of their kind.

We cannot, moreover, follow Voigt in supposing the *actio ex stipulatu* to have been expressly invented for *fidepromissio* and *cautio rei uxoriae.* We have to presuppose the existence of a *condictio incerti* before the *doli clausula* could become actionable, since a claim of damages for *dolus* was necessarily an *incertum*; and there is no reason why the *actio ex stipulatu* should not have been developed from the *condictio incerti* by mere interpretation. Its essential connection with the *stipulatio* containing the *clausula doli* may readily be admitted, but we cannot be certain what were the first stipulations containing *clausulae* of the kind.

The *doli clausulae* are well summarized by Voigt[6] as follows :

[1] *I. N.* iv. 413.   [2] *I. N.* iv. 407.

[3] Boeth. *ad Top.* 17. 66.   [4] 23 *Dig.* 4. 26.

[5] 45 *Dig.* 1. 122.   [6] *I. N.* iv. 411.

(i) "*Quod melius aequius erit*," as in "*cautio rei uxoriae*."

(ii) "*Fide*," in *fidepromissio*.

(iii) "*Si quid dolo in ea re factum sit*[1]."

(iv) "*Dolum malum huic rei abesse afuturumque esse spondesne*[2] *?*"

(v) "*Cui rei si dolus malus non abest, non abfuerit, quanti ea res est tantam pecuniam dari spondes*[3] *?* "

The date of each of these forms is, however, impossible to determine. The cases of contracts by stipulation in which *doli clausulae* are found have been collected by Voigt[4], but need not be enumerated here.

The effect of the *clausula* was to convert the action on the stipulation containing it from a *stricti iuris* action into a *bonae fidei* action, in which equitable defences might be entertained by the judge. This expansion was effected by introducing the words "*dare facere oportere ex fide bona* " in the *intentio* of the action. If "*ex fide bona* " had not appeared in the formula of an *actio ex stipulatu*, the action would simply have been a *condictio incerti*. It seems therefore reasonable to suppose that the *actio ex stipulatu* was nothing more than a development of the *condictio incerti*, and that the words *ex fide bona*, perhaps suggested by the *actio emti*, were inserted to suit the liberal language of the stipulation.

In praetorian stipulations the *doli clausula* was

[1] 4 *Dig.* 8. 31.
[2] 46 *Dig.* 7. 19, 50 *Dig.* 16. 69.
[3] 45 *Dig.* 1. 38. fr. 13.
[4] *I. N.* IV. 416 ff.

an usual part of the formula; e.g. in *cautio legis Falcidiae*[1], *stipulatio iudicatum solui*[2], *stipulatio ratam rem haberi*[3], etc. But in conventional stipulations it was purely a matter of choice whether the *doli clausula* should be inserted or not.

We must not fancy that the *actio de dolo* and the *exceptio doli,* which Cicero attributes to his colleague C. Aquilius Gallus[4], had anything in common with the *actio ex stipulatu* based upon a *clausula doli*[5]. The former remedies were a protection against fraud where no agreement of a contrary kind had been made[6], whereas the action on a stipulation containing the *clausula doli* was available only when *dolus malus* had been specially excluded by agreement. Hence it follows that where the stipulation had omitted the *clausula doli* there can have been no remedy for *dolus* until the great reform introduced by Aquilius Gallus.

As soon as stipulations of all kinds had thus become actionable, and had probably passed out of the hands of the Pontiffs into the far more popular jurisdiction of the Praetor, the law of contract received an extraordinary stimulus, and we find the stipulation producing entirely new varieties of obligation, though its form in each kind of contract remained of course substantially the same. Here are some of the purposes for which *stipulatio* was em-

---

[1] 35 *Dig.* 3. 1. [2] 46 *Dig.* 1. 33.

[3] 46 *Dig.* 8. 22. fr. 7.

[4] *Off.* III. 14. 60. *Nat. D.* III. 30. 74.

[5] Voigt, *I. N.* 3. 319.

[6] See the case of *Canius*, in Cic. *Off.* III. 14. 58–60.

ployed, apart from its uses in procedure and surety-ship.

(1) It produced a special form of agency by means of *adstipulatio*[1]. The promisee who wished a claim of his to be satisfied at some far-off period, when he might himself be dead, had only to get a friend to join with him in receiving the stipulatory promise. This friend could then at any time prosecute the claim with as good right as the principal *stipulator*, and the law recognised him as agent for the latter. Even a slave could in this way stipulate on behalf of his master[2].

(2) In consequence of its universal adaptability, the stipulation gave rise to *nouatio*. The reducing to a simple verbal obligation of some debt or obligation based upon different grounds (e.g. upon a sale, legacy, etc.) was accomplished by *stipulatio*, and known as *expromissio debiti proprii*.

(3) It created a rudimentary assignability of obligations by virtue of *delegatio*, another form of *nouatio*. In the one case, the debtor was changed, and the creditor was authorised by the former debtor to stipulate from the new debtor the amount of the former debt: in the other case (*expromissio debiti alieni*) the creditor was changed, and the new creditor stipulated from the debtor the amount owed by him to the former creditor.

(4) It also created the notion of correal obligation, by which two or more promisors in a stipulation made themselves jointly responsible for the whole debt, and so gave additional security to

[1] Gai. III. 117.   [2] 3 *Inst.* 17. 1.

the promisee. The effects of this will be seen in a later section.

(5) It served to embody in a convenient shape any special condition annexed to a separate contract —e.g. a promise to pay the price agreed upon in a sale[1], and the *stipulationes simplae et duplae* annexed to sales of *res nec mancipi*[2]. Thus an enforceable *contractus adiectus* could be made on the analogy of a *pactum adiectum*.

(6) It clothed in an actionable form so many different kinds of agreements that it would be impossible to exhaust the list. For instance, agreements as to interest[3], wagers, the promise of a dowry[4], the making of a compromise[5], the creation of an usufruct, could all be thrown into stipulations either single or reciprocal, and thus turned into binding obligations.

(7) Most of the events in the history of this immense development of *stipulatio* are impossible to fix at any given period, though the attempt to do so has been often made. Yet the invention of one famous stipulation can be exactly dated, from its bearing the name of Cicero's colleague, C. Aquilius Gallus, and having therefore been invented by him in the year of his Praetorship[6]. This Aquilian formula, which operated as a general release of all obligations, and which the Institutes[7] give us in full, is an excellent instance of the usefulness of the stipulation, and it also clearly shows what long and

[1] Cato, *R. R.* 146.   [2] Varro, *R. R.* II. 3.
[3] Plaut. *Most.* 3. 1. 101.   [4] See p. 32.
[5] Plaut. *Bacch.* 4. 8. 76.   [6] A.V.C. 688.   [7] 3 *Inst.* 29. 2.

elaborate forms this contract sometimes assumed in later times, so that all kinds of terms, descriptions or warranties might without difficulty be incorporated in a single comprehensive formula. It was probably this increasing length of stipulations which caused them to be put in writing, and induced lawyers to publish *formulae* in which they should be expressed. Both of these results had already taken place in the time of Cicero. He not only speaks of written stipulations,- but also describes the composition of stipulatory formulae as one of the chief literary occupations of a leading lawyer[1]. We know from a constitution of the Emperor Leo, which changed the law in this respect, that the written stipulations of the Republic and early Empire were merely put into writing for the sake of evidence[2]. The writing in itself constituted no contract, and raised no presumption in favour of the existence of a contract; but the written stipulation had to conform with all the rules of the ordinary spoken stipulation, since it was nothing but a spoken stipulation recorded in writing.

The legislative changes of the period were mostly devoted to modifications in the stipulations of suretyship. But in a few cases the ordinary stipulation was itself affected.

(i) By the *Lex Titia* of A.V.C. 416—426[3] stipulations for the payment of money lost at gambling were declared void.

(ii) Various laws against usury were enacted,

---

[1] *de leg.* I. 4. 14.   [2] *3 Inst.* 15. 1.

[3] Voigt in *Phil. Hist. Ber. der S. G. der W.* XIII. 257.

all of which affected the stipulation, since that was the mode in which *fenus* was usually contracted.

(iii) The *Lex Cincia de muneribus* of A. V. C. 550, the object of which was to restrain lavish gifts to pleaders and public men, naturally limited all stipulations between parties within range of the prohibition, and in the corresponding *condictio* gave rise to the *exceptio legis Cinciae*, which probably ran thus: *...si in ea re nihil contra legem Cinciam factum sit....*

(iv) The Praetor C. Aquilius Gallus, as above mentioned[1], instituted in his Edict the *exceptio doli mali*, and thereby nullified stipulations which, however perfect in form, had been procured by fraud. This *exceptio* was of course inapplicable to cases in which the stipulation contained a *clausula doli*.

II. *Sponsio in the law of Procedure.*

The original function of the processual *sponsio* seems to have been that of helping to decide the question at issue by expressing it in the form of a wager. As a common feature of practice, *sponsio* made its appearance in many other different connections, and sometimes developed into the more modern *stipulatio*. We find it employed:

(i) As a means of obtaining a decision by a wager, in which the contention of either party was succinctly stated and so submitted to the judge. This was known as *sponsio praeiudicialis*.

(ii) As a means of fixing a penalty, as well as of obtaining a decision, in (*a*) the *condictio certae*

---

[1] p. 109.

pecuniae or (*b*) the interdicts, in which case it was known as *sponsio poenalis*.

(iii) As a mode of giving security; for instance in the *uindicatio*, where we find the *stipulatio pro praede litis et uindiciarum*.

Bekker's classification[1] does not exactly correspond with this one. He divides processual *sponsiones* into (A) *sponsiones* made in the course of a trial,

(*a*) as to the chief question,

(*b*) as to conditions and incidental matters,

and (B) *sponsiones* made apart from a trial,

(*a*) with a view to some future trial,

(*b*) with no such view.

The objection to this classification seems to be that the whole of class (B) were not properly processual *sponsiones* at all.

1. *Sponsio praeiudicialis*[2] was a promise to pay a fixed sum, made by the plaintiff to the defendant, and conditioned upon the plaintiff's defeat. It was accompanied by a similar promise (*restipulatio*) on the part of the defendant, conditioned upon his defeat. These mutual *sponsiones* were in fact nothing more than a bet on the result of the action. They generally involved a merely nominal sum, and were perhaps first introduced in the *actio per sponsionem in rem*, as a means of settling the question of ownership without employing the larger and more costly *sacramentum* of five hundred *asses*[3]. The date of their origin is impossible to fix, but the custom of making such *sponsiones* and having them decided by a judge

[1] *Akt.* I. 257.   [2] Gai. IV. 94. 165.

[3] Baron, p. 403.

seems to have been one of great antiquity, and must have existed long before the *sponsio* became armed with any *condictio*. The very notion of a bet submitted to a judge as a means of deciding rights of property seems, as Sir Henry Maine has said[1], to savour of the primitive time when the judge was simply a man of wisdom called in to arbitrate between two disputants. Moreover, it is hard to imagine that the *actio per sponsionem in rem* could have been introduced in any but the most ancient times, when in Cicero's age there were the *rei uindicatio sacramento* and the far simpler *rei uindicatio per formulam petitoriam* to accomplish the same object[2]. There is therefore every probability that the *actio per sponsionem* was at least as old as the *legis actio sacramento*. According to Voigt[3] the procedure *per sponsionem* was the original form also of the *actio Publiciana* introduced in A.V.C. 519. In Cicero's time it was still a favorite method of procedure for all sorts of litigation[4].

(*a*) In questions as to property the plaintiff might choose whether he preferred to bring an *actio per formulam petitoriam* or one *per sponsionem*[5]. If he chose the latter course, the defendant was compelled *sponsione se defendere*.

(*b*) In really trivial *praeiudicia* the question was stated in the formula and sent straight to the *iudex* without any *condemnatio*[6], but the procedure

---

[1] *E. H. of I.* 259.

[2] Keller, *C. P.* § 28.   [3] *I. N.* IV. 506.   [4] e.g. *Caec.* 8.

[5] *Lex Rubr.* c. 21, 22; Cic. 2 *Verr.* I. 45. 115; Gaius, IV. 91.

[6] Gai. IV. 44.

in this case was not necessarily based upon a *sponsio praeiudicialis* and might be a simple preliminary inquiry ordered by the Praetor.

The *sponsio praeiudicialis* thus worked in a peculiarly roundabout way; its penalty was nominal and not therefore its real object, and it brought about a decision on the main question by treating that question as a thing of secondary importance.

2. *Sponsio poenalis* (*a*) in the *condictio*, was peculiar to the *legis actio per condictionem* introduced by the *Lex Silia*. It was accompanied by a *restipulatio*, so that either party to the action promised to the other a penalty of one-third[1] in the event of losing his case. Rudorff[2] reconstructs the formula of this *sponsio* as follows : *Si pecuniam certam creditam qua de re agitur mihi debes, eam pecuniam cum tertia parte amplius dare spondes?* But this seems incorrect, since from Cicero's language[3] we gather that the *sponsio* was for the *tertia pars* only ; the sum in dispute plus one-third is never mentioned. The formula then was probably as follows : *Si pecuniam certam creditam qua de agitur mihi debes, eius pecuniae tertiam partem dare spondes?* Hence Rudorff[4] seems also wrong in stating that the *condemnatio* of the formula in the corresponding *condictio* must have involved the principal sum plus one-third. Voigt[5] more correctly holds that the *condemnatio* can only have involved the *summa sponsionis*. We can

---

[1] Cic. *Rosc. Com.* 5. 14.   [2] *Ed. Perp.* p. 103.

[3] "*legitimae partis sponsio facta est.*" *Rosc. Com.* 4. 10.

[4] *Röm. RG.* II. 142.   [5] *I. N.* III. 741.

see that, as Gaius[1] implies, this *sponsio* was just as much *praeiudicialis* as that of the *actio per sponsionem,* giving as it did a ground for the decision of the main question ; but it was also distinctly *poenalis,* because the sum which it involved was worth having and worth extorting from the unsuccessful party, and therefore the *condemnatio* was carried out in the usual manner. The principal sum in dispute was then no doubt quietly paid, since the decision as to the *sponsio tertiae partis* had also settled to whom the disputed sum belonged.

(*b*) In the private interdicts (*possessoria* and *restitutoria*) if the party to whom the interdict was addressed chose to dispute it, he might do so by challenging the plaintiff to make a *sponsio* and *restipulatio,* the rights of which should be determined by *recuperatores.* This *sponsio* differed from the former (1) by being purely *poenalis* and having no trace of *praeiudicium* for its object; (2) by being *in factum concepta*[2].

The origin of these two uses of *sponsio* cannot be dated, in the case of (*a*) because we do not know the date of the *Lex Silia,* and in the case of (*b*) because we do not know when the possessory interdict was first granted by the Praetor. But it is fairly certain that the *sponsio poenalis* of the interdict was more modern than the *sponsio poenalis* of the *condictio,* partly because it had no sort of connection with a *praeiudicium,* which seems to have been the original object of the processual *sponsio,* and partly because it was *in factum concepta.*

[1] IV. 93, 94. [2] Gai. IV. 166; Cic. *Caec.* 8. 23.

3. Another purpose for which the *sponsio* was adopted in procedure was to give bond against possible losses. It thus furnished a substitute for the old form of obligation contracted by the *praes* in real actions. The *stipulatio pro praede litis et uindiciarum*, accompanied by sureties[1], was given by the plaintiff who wished to bring an *actio per sponsionem in rem*, or who disputed an interdict, and the amount promised in the stipulation was double the value of the property in dispute.

Another contract of the same kind was the *stipulatio iudicatum solui*[2], by which the plaintiff in an *actio per formulam petitoriam* obtained a promise from the defendant that he would pay up the value of the property in dispute and of its *fructus*, in the event of being defeated in the action.

Voigt gives imaginary formulae for these two stipulations[3], but in reality we do not know much about them. Stipulations of this kind were not peculiar to the law of procedure. They were simply varieties of the *cautio*, a very common method of securing future rights, and they had their counterpart in the *cautio damni infecti, cautio Muciana, cautio legis Falcidiae* and all the praetorian stipulations. The origin of the *cautiones* in general cannot however be dated: we know merely that they must have been invented subsequently to the introduction of the *condictio*.

III. *Sponsio as a means of Suretyship.*

The introduction of the new idea of correal obli-

---

[1] Cic. 2 *Verr.* I. 45. 115; Gai. IV. 91–94.
[2] 46 *Dig.* 7. 20; Gai. IV. 89.   [3] *Ius Nat.* III. 588 and 820.

gation which resulted from the use of the stipulation, naturally led to the use of the stipulation as a mode of suretyship. For if three *sponsores* promised the same sum to the same *stipulator*, the latter obviously had three times as good security as if he had put his question to one *sponsor* instead of to three.

1. The consequence was that *sponsor* soon acquired the special meaning of a co-promisor or surety, and this change probably took place soon after the *sponsio* became actionable by the *Lex Silia*. But if the surety-*sponsor* had had no recourse against the principal-*sponsor* whose debt he had been compelled to satisfy, his case would have been hard indeed. To provide against this hardship, the *Lex Publilia* [1] of A. V. C. 427 enacted:

(*a*) That the surety-*sponsor* might make use of an *actio depensi* against the principal debtor for the amount spent on his behalf.

(*b*) That the mode of procedure in this *actio depensi* should be the *legis actio per manus iniectionem*, and that the penalty should be *duplum* [2].

(*c*) That the principal debtor should however have six months' grace for the repayment of his surety, but

(*d*) That a surety who paid a gambling-debt on behalf of his principal should forfeit his right of action.

This law is alluded to by Plautus, and was clearly prior to the introduction of *fidepromissio*.

---

[1] Voigt in *Phil. Hist. Ber. der k. s. Ges. d. Wiss.* XLII. p. 259.

[2] Gai. IV. 22. 171.

In later times the surety had in the *actio mandati* a further remedy against the principal *sponsor*.

2. About the beginning of the fifth century, as new forms of *stipulatio* grew up alongside of the old *sponsio*, another sort of suretyship was introduced under the name of *fidepromissio*. It was so called because the sureties entered into a stipulation containing the words: "*fide tua promittis? fide mea promitto.*" The new form was no doubt devised for the benefit of foreigners and marked the further growth of *ius gentium*. It seems to have been treated as exactly equivalent to *sponsio*, for *sponsio* as well as *fidepromissio* could only be used to secure a verbal obligation[1]. Since it is coupled with *sponsio* in the *Lex Apuleia*, and since the heirs of *sponsores* and *fidepromissores* were both alike free from the obligation of their predecessors[2], it is fairly certain that the *actio depensi* and *manus iniectio* of the *Lex Publilia* must have been extended to *fidepromissio* by interpretation[3]. The *fidepromissor* also had the remedy of the *actio mandati*, but this was of later origin.

The *Lex Apuleia de sponsoribus et fide promissoribus* of A.V.C. 525[4], applying to both Italy and the provinces, gave to any *sponsor* or *fidepromissor* who had paid more than his aliquot share of the principal debt a right to bring the severe *actio depensi* against each of his co-promisors to recover the amount overpaid. This law, giving as it did protection to the *sponsor* against his co-sponsor, was

[1] Gai. III. 119; IV. 137.   [2] Gai. III. 120.
[3] Gai. III. 127.   [4] Voigt, *I. N.* IV. 424.

the natural complement to the *Lex Publilia* which had already secured him against the principal debtor.

The object of the next law, *Lex Furia de sponsoribus et fidepromissoribus* of A.V.C. 536[1], is rather obscure, but it seems to have re-enacted the *Lex Apuleia* with reference to Italy only, and probably provided the *sponsor* with a more thorough mode of redress. What this mode was the language of Gaius[2] does not make plain; but Moyle is no doubt wrong in asserting [3] that it was the *actio pro socio*, unmistakably of much later origin. Its only clearly new enactment was that *sponsores* or *fidepromissores* in Italy, whose guarantee was for an unlimited period, should be liable for two years only. This limited liability Voigt thinks was perhaps borrowed from the rules applying to the *uas*.

Lastly, the *Lex Cicereia* (Studemund) of uncertain date, but which must have been passed before A.V.C. 620, since it ignored *fideiussio*, gave further protection to sureties by enacting:

(*a*) That any creditor who secured his debt by taking *sponsores* or *fidepromissores* must announce the amount of the debt and the number of the sureties before they gave their *adpromissio*.

(*b*) If he failed to do this, any surety might within 30 days institute a *praeiudicium* to inquire into his conduct; and if the judge declared that the required announcement had not been made, all the sureties were freed from their liability[4]. This law

---

[1] L. Furius Philus was Praetor in that year. Voigt, *I. N.* iv. 424.
[2] III. 122.   [3] *Inst.* p. 411, note.   [4] Gai. III. 123.

was subsequently, we know, extended by interpretation to *fideiussores*.

3. A third form of suretyship was at last devised, by which obligations other than verbal ones could be similarly secured. This was done by a stipulation containing the words " *fide tua iubes ? fide mea iubeo*," and it was hence known as *fideiussio*. It must have been invented about the beginning of the sixth century, and was doubtless needed, as Voigt suggests [1], in order to provide a form of suretyship for the newly invented real and consensual contracts [2]. Its chief points of difference from the other two forms were that (*a*) it applied to all kinds of contractual obligations; (*b*) the heir of the *fideiussor* was bound by the same obligation as his predecessor; and (*c*) the provisions of the foregoing legislation as to *sponsio* and *fidepromissio* did not as a rule apply to *fideiussio*. The only point of resemblance was that the *fideiussor*, like the *sponsor* and *fidepromissor*, had the *actio mandati* [3] against his principal, whereas the *sponsor* and probably the *fidepromissor* had the *actio depensi* of the *Lex Publilia* in addition to the more modern remedy.

The *Lex Cornelia* mentioned by Gaius [4] as affecting all sureties alike, whether *sponsores, fidepromissores* or *fideiussores,* has been shown by Voigt [5] to be a part of the *Lex Cornelia sumtuaria* of A.V.C. 673. Two sections of this act provided :

(i) That no surety should validly become re-

---

[1] *I. N.* IV. 425.   [2] Gai. III. 119.
[3] Gai. III. 127.   [4] III. 124.
[5] *Phil. Hist. Ber. der k. s. Ges. der Wiss.* XLII. p. 280.

sponsible for more than two million sesterces[1] on behalf of the same person in any given year. Except in the case of *dos*[2], whatever liability was contracted over and above that amount was void.

(ii) That no suretyship of any sort should be valid when given for a gambling debt[3].

In thus tabulating all the laws on this subject, we must not omit to mention the rule applying to all forms of suretyship alike, that if the surety had guaranteed a lesser sum than the principal debt, his guarantee held good, but if a larger sum or a different thing, the guarantee became void.

In conclusion, it is very remarkable how largely the law of suretyship was developed by means of legislation. The reason was, that while sufficient means existed for enforcing the mutual obligations of debtor and creditor, there were no rules to regulate the relations of debtor and surety, or of sureties among one another. The old *uadimonium* was apparently inadequate, while the newer *uadimonium*, as we saw, was but a form of *stipulatio*, and the ordinary *condictio* would clearly have been inapplicable to cases of this kind. Hence it became necessary that legislation should intervene.

Art. 3. EXPENSILATIO. So many irreconcilable statements have been made as to the nature of this peculiarly Roman contract[4] that no one can hope to describe it with perfect accuracy. Confident

---

[1] 20,000 according to Danz, *R. RG.* ii. 83.

[2] Gai. iii. 124–5.   [3] Voigt, *Röm. RG.* i. 616.

[4] See a full summary of the various opinions in Danz, *R. RG.* ii. pp. 43–60.

assertions on the subject serve only to show our real ignorance, and ignorant we must be, owing to the vagueness of the evidence. Yet it is only as to the form of the contract that much controversy has prevailed. Its operation and its history are tolerably certain.

Form: Our ignorance respecting the mode in which the contract was made is partly due to the fact that *tabulae,* which meant account-books in general, meant also a chirograph, or a written stipulation, or an ordinary note-book [1]. We can never be quite sure in what sense a technical term of such ambiguity is used in any given passage. Everyone agrees that the entry of a debt in the creditor's account-book imposed a corresponding obligation upon the debtor, and the theory that debts were entered for this purpose in separate documents has been exploded ever since Savigny [2] refuted it. But the question so difficult to answer is this: what sort of account-book was the *codex* in which these binding entries were made ? We gather from Cicero's speech for Roscius the actor that there were in his day at least two principal books in general use, (1) *aduersaria* [3], and (2) *codex* or *tabulae rationum.* The former was a day-book, in which the details of every-day business were jotted down, while the latter was a carefully kept ledger, containing a summary of the household receipts and expenditure, copied at regular intervals from the *aduersaria.* These two

---

[1] See Wunderlich, *Litt. oblig.* p. 19.

[2] *Verm. Schrif.* I. 211 ff.

[3] Also called *ephemeris,* Prop. III. 23. 20.

THEORIES OF BOOK-KEEPING.

books were also used by bankers (*argentarii*); and in
their *codex* or ledger were entered their accounts-
current with their different customers [1]. Similarly in
the *codex* of the householder there were probably
separate accounts, on separate folios, under such
heads as *ratio praedii, ratio loculorum*, &c.[2] There
was sometimes used a book known as (3) *kalendarium*,
in which the interest on loans was computed and
entered [3], the making of loans at interest being
hence called *kalendarium exercere*.

(*a*) Some writers are of opinion that these
book-debts were entered by the creditor in the main
codex, and that this *codex* was a mere cash-book.
In that case, unless the debt was a loan actually
paid in cash, it must have been entered on both
sides of the account, debtor as well as creditor,
otherwise the book would not have balanced. This
twofold entry is said to have been called *transcriptio*;
and *nomen transcripticium* would accordingly have
been the name applied to any debt contracted in
that manner. The weakness of this theory lies in the
clumsiness of the alleged twofold method of entry;
we can scarcely believe that an imaginary receipt
would have been credited in the account simply
for the purpose of making both sides balance. Moreover it is unwise to assume, as these writers do
in support of their theory, that the Roman method
of keeping accounts was an easy matter and therefore
needed but few books; for in a large town house, or
on a large estate with bailiffs, tenants and slaves to

[1] 2 *Dig.* 13. 10 and 2 *Dig.* 14. 47.   [2] 33 *Dig.* 8. 23.
[3] 12 *Dig.* 1. 41 and 33 *Dig.* 8. 23.

be provided for, it seems far more likely that the accounts should have been elaborate and the account-books numerous.

(*b*) According to Voigt, book-debts (*nomina*) were entered in a (4) *codex accepti et expensi* kept for the express purpose. Whether such a fourth book existed, or whether the *rationes accepti et expensi* were kept as a separate account in the main *codex rationum*, is a question which our authorities hardly enable us to answer. This does not however seem very important, and it is certainly impossible to tell in any given passage whether the author is speaking of the main *codex* (2), or of the *codex accepti et expensi* (4), which Voigt supposes to have been a distinct book. His theory is plausible, for *codex accepti et expensi* would be a very natural name for a book containing only *expensa lata* and *accepta lata*. But we may fairly doubt the existence of this fourth book, partly because there is no passage which clearly distinguishes it from the other account-books, and partly because it is hard to see why the books of a Roman household, though clearly numerous, should have been thus needlessly multiplied. Why should not '*nomina facere*[1]' have meant "to open an account" with a man, and why could not such an account have been opened as well on a folio of the principal ledger as on a folio of the imaginary *codex accepti et expensi*? Perhaps a banker may have found it worth his while to keep, as Voigt supposes, a separate book for his loans and book-debts, but we

---

[1] Cic. 2 *Verr.* i. 36. 92 ; Seneca, *Ben.* iii. 15.

cannot imagine that this would have been the common practice of ordinary householders, when their *codex* would have done equally well.

Expensilatio was the name of the transaction, while the entry itself was called *nomen*; and the term *nomen transcripticium*, which has been explained as the equivalent of *nomen*, because the entry was transcribed from the *aduersaria* into the *codex*, or because it was copied into both sides of the account, seems rather to have denoted only a *nomen* of a novatory character[1]. That *nomen* could produce an original obligation is proved by the cases of Visellius Varro[2] and of Canius[3] in which there is no mention of *transcriptio*. Further Gaius clearly implies[4] that the *nomen transcripticium* was but one instance of the use of *expensilatio*, and the cases cited by him are purely novatory. Voigt therefore is probably right in distinguishing the ordinary *nomen* which created an obligation, from the *nomen transcripticium* which novated an obligation already existent. If so, the name *transcripticium* comes from the fact that

(*a*) a debt entered in one place as owed by Titius might be *transcribed* into another part of the *codex* as owed by Negidius (*transcriptio a persona in personam*), or

(*b*) a debt owed by Negidius, on account of (e.g.) a sale, might be embodied in an *expensilatio* and thus *converted* from a *bonae fidei* into a *stricti iuris*

[1] See Gaius III. 128. [2] Val. Max. VIII. 2. 2.
[3] Cic. *Off.* III. 14. 59.
[4] "*ueluti nominibus transcripticiis*," III. 130.

obligation by being entered in the *codex* (*transcriptio a re in personam*).

Some passages are supposed to describe the entry of book-debts in the books not only of the debtor and creditor, but of third persons also[1]; but it is difficult to imagine that any man would have entered in the midst of his own accounts a record of transactions which did not actually concern him. Here again we may believe that the ambiguity of the word *tabulae* has led the commentators astray. What they have taken for the account-books of a third party may have meant simply his memorandum or note-book. Salpius[2] has endeavoured to explain away the difficulty by asserting that these *tabulae* of third parties really mean in every instance the *tabulae* of either debtor or creditor. But the passages do not seem to be capable of bearing such an interpretation, and it appears far more likely that the word *tabulae* has caused all the difficulty.

To summarise then this view of the Literal Contract, we may believe it to have been made by an entry written by the creditor on a separate folio of the *codex* (2) or chief household ledger, and that its form was very probably that given by Voigt[3] as follows :

"*HS X a Numerio Negidio promissa &c. expensa Numerio Negidio fero in diem*" *;* whereupon the debtor might, if he liked, make this corresponding entry in his codex: "*HS X Aulo Agerio promissa &c., Aulo Agerio refero in diem.*"

---

[1] E.g. Cic. *Att.* IV. 18; *Rosc. Com.* I. 1; *de Or.* II. 69. 280.
[2] *Novation*, p. 95. [3] *Röm. RG.* I. 64.

In cases of novation, the form would be as follows:
Creditor: *"HS X a Lucio Titio debita expensa Numerio Negidio fero in diem"* (*transcriptio a persona in personam*), or else: *"HS X a Numerio Negidio ex emti causa debita expensa Numerio Negidio fero in diem"* (*transcriptio a re in personam*). As in the previous case, the debtor might make similar entries in his *codex.*

Having thus opened an account, which could only be done with the authorisation of the debtor, the creditor would naturally enter on the same page such items as payment of interest on the debt, payment of the principal on account, &c. According to Voigt, the entries showing repayment of the principal would be made in the following form: *"HS X a Numerio Negidio debita accepta Numerio Negidio fero."* Such an entry constituted a valid release and went by the name of *acceptilatio.* Voigt[1] thinks that the *acceptilatio,* as here given, was made first by the debtor, and that the creditor followed him with a corresponding *accepti relatio.* But the word *acceptum* seems rather to imply that the release was looked upon from the creditor's point of view. It is therefore more likely to have been the creditor who took the initiative in entering the *acceptilatio,* just as he did in entering the *expensilatio,* while the debtor perhaps followed him with an *accepti relatio.*

We know from Cicero[2] that *expensilatio* could be used to create an original obligation, while Gaius tells us that it was much used for making an assignment or a novation. Where however a loan made in

---

[1] *ib.* p. 65.   [2] *Off.* III. 14. 58–60.

cash was entered in the creditor's book, the contract was regarded as a case not of *expensilatio* but of *mutuum*, and the entry was called *nomen arcarium*[1]. This name seems to have come from the fact that the money was actually drawn from the *arca* or money-chest[2]; and in such case the entry on the creditor's books constituted no fresh obligation, but served merely as evidence of the *mutuum*.

History : The old theory of its origin, given by Savigny and Sir Henry Maine, is that *expensilatio* was a simplified form of *nexum*. They argued that the word *expensum* pointed clearly to the fiction of a money-loan made by weight. But they never succeeded in explaining how it happened that the nexal loan should have produced a contract so strangely different from itself.

The newer theory, which Voigt has ably set forth[3], is far more intelligible and agrees with all the facts. Its merit lies in recognising *expensilatio* as a device first used by bankers and merchants and subsequently adopted by the rest of the community. Nothing indeed could be plainer than the commercial origin of *expensilatio*. Like the negotiable instrument of modern times it is a striking instance of the extent to which Trade has moulded the Law of Contract. This institution probably did not originate at Rome, but the Greek bankers of Southern Italy may have adopted and used it centuries before we hear of its existence. It seems to have been first introduced[4] by the Greek *argen-*

[1] Gaius III. 131.
[2] Cic. *Top.* 3. 16.
[3] *I. N.* II. 244 ff.
[4] Voigt, *Röm. RG.* I. 60.

tarii or *tarpezitae* (τραπεζῖται), who came to Rome
about A. V. C. 410—440, and took the seven shops
known as *tabernae ueteres*[1] on the East side of the
Forum[2]. Their numbers were subsequently increased,
when the *tabernae nouae* were also occupied by them.
Their business was extremely varied and their system
of book-keeping doubtless highly developed. They
made loans[3], received deposits[4], cashed cheques
(*perscriptiones*)[5], managed auctions[6], and exchanged
foreign monies for a commission (*collybus*)[7]. They
also used *codices accepti et expensi*, in which, as we
have seen, accounts-current were kept with their
customers[8]. We learn from Livy[9] that by A. V. C.
559 the *expensilatio* thus introduced by them had
become a common transaction among private individuals. It cannot have been long before the
conception of *pecunia credita* was extended so as
to cover book-debts as well as stipulations; but
we do not know the exact date. From Cicero[10]
however we learn that *pecunia expensa lata* was a
branch of *pecunia credita* within the scope of the
Lex Silia, and that the proper remedy for its
enforcement was the *condictio certae pecuniae* with
its *sponsio tertiae partis.* As Voigt[11] has well
pointed out, the *expensilatio* presupposes the existence throughout the community of a high standard
of good faith. It was therefore ill adapted for

[1] Liu. xxvi. 27. [2] Liu. vii. 21.
[3] Plaut. *Curc.* 5. 2. 20. [4] *ib.* 2. 3. 66.
[5] *ib.* 3. 62–65. [6] Cic. *Caec.* 6. 16.
[7] Cic. *Att.* xii. 6. 1. [8] 2 *Dig.* 14. 47.
[9] Liu. xxxv. 7. [10] *Rosc. Com.* 5. 14.
[11] *I. N.* ii. 420.

general use among the Greeks, whose bad faith was proverbial[1]. The fact that it was at Rome, and at Rome only, that this contract received full legal recognition, is proved by Gaius' doubts[2] as to whether a peregrin could be bound by a *nomen transcripticium*. By the end of the Republic *expensilatio* was at its height of favour, but it died out, except among bankers, soon after the time of Gaius, for in Justinian's day it was unknown.

Art. 4. CHIROGRAPHVM and SYNGRAPHA were forms of written contract borrowed, as their name implies, from Greek custom, and chiefly used by peregrins, as Gaius informs us[3]. The distinction between the two was purely formal, the one being signed by the debtor (*chirographum*), and the other being written out in duplicate, signed by both parties, and kept by each of them (*syngrapha*)[4]. These foreign instruments at first produced nothing more than a *pactum nudum*, for wherever we find *syngrapha* mentioned in Plautus, it denotes a mere agreement (*pactum*), the terms of which had been committed to writing and which was certainly not actionable, while *chirographum* never occurs in his plays. The Roman magistrates, finding these instruments recognised by aliens, ventured at length to enforce debts *ex syngrapha*, and thus their legal validity was secured[5]. They had received some sort of recognition by the

[1] Plaut. *Asin.* 1. 3. 47.

[2] III. 133.　　　　　　[3] III. 134.

[4] See Dict. thirteenth cent. in Heimbach, *Creditum* p. 520, and Ascon. *in Cic. Verr.* I. 36.

[5] Cic. *pro Rab. Post.* 3. 6; *Har. resp.* 13. 29; *Phil.* II. 37. 95; *ad Att.* VI. 1. 15; *ib.* v. 21. 10; *ib.* VI. 2. 7.

time of Cicero, but when they were first enforced does not appear, though it was certainly late in the history of the Republic. Gneist[1] has advanced the theory that in Cicero's time neither *chirographum* nor *syngrapha* was a genuine literal contract, but only a document attesting the fact of a loan, which could always be rebutted by evidence *aliunde*. This theory is the more plausible because Gaius himself does not seem certain as to the binding nature of these documents[2].

An interesting passage in Theophilus[3] is sometimes said to give the form in which *litterarum obligatio* proper, i.e. *expensilatio*, was contracted. This view is certainly wrong, for the context shows that Theophilus meant to describe a contract signed by the creditor and known as *chirographum*. As a sample of how *chirographa* were made, the Latin translation of this instrument may therefore be quoted: " *Centum aureos quos mihi ex caussa locationis debes tu ex conuentione et confessione litterarum tuarum dabis?*" And to this the debtor wrote the following answer: " *Ex conuentione debeo litterarum mearum.*" This was evidently not a *nomen transcripticium*, but a *chirographum* or *syngrapha*, since Gaius expressly states *debere se aut daturum se scribere* to be the usual phraseology of such instruments. Both parties also seem here to have been present, whereas one of the chief advantages of *expensilatio* was that it enabled debts (by *expensilatio*) and assignments (by *transcriptio*) to be validly made without requiring the presence of the parties

---

[1] *Form. Vertr.* p. 113.   [2] III. 134.   [3] *Paraphr.* III. 21.

concerned. Heimbach[1] is therefore wrong in taking the above passage as equivalent to " *Expensos tibi tuli ?*" " *Expensos mihi tulisti.*" The transaction was evidently different from *expensilatio*, and can have been nothing else than a *chirographum*. Another specimen *chirographum* preserved in the Digest[2] shows that the promise or acknowledgement was sometimes made in a letter from the debtor to the creditor.

---

[1] *Cred.* p. 330. [2] 2 *Dig.* 14. 47.

CHAPTER VI.

CONTRACTS OF THE IVS GENTIVM. *Part I.*

Consensual Contracts.

Art. 1. EMTIO VENDITIO. The forms of contract hitherto examined have been distinguished from most of the contracts of modern law in one or more of the following respects :

(i)   They were confined to Roman citizens.

(ii)   They were unilateral.

(iii)   They were capable of imposing obligations only by virtue of some particular formality.

(iv)   They were available only *inter praesentes.*

The contract which we are now about to consider was modern in all its aspects :

(i)   It was open to aliens as well as to citizens.

(ii)   It was bi-lateral.

(iii)   It rested only upon the consent of the parties, required no formality, and could be resolved like any modern contract into a proposal by one party [1] which became a contract when accepted by the other party.

---

[1] Plaut. *Epid.* 3. 4. 35.

(iv) It could be made at any distance, provided
the parties clearly understood one another's meaning.

How then can the formal contracts of the older
law ever have produced such a modern institution to
all outward appearance as the consensual contract of
sale ?

The elements which make up the popular conception of sale are usually fourfold ; they consist of:

(1) The agreement by which buyer and seller
determine to exchange the wares of the latter for
the money of the former ;

(2) The transfer of the wares from the seller to
the buyer ;

(3) The payment of the price by the buyer to
the seller ;

(4) The representation, express or implied, of
the seller to the buyer, that his wares are as good in
point of quantity or quality as they are understood
to be.

Mancipatio was at first a combination of the
second and third elements above-mentioned.   It
was a transfer of ownership followed by an immediate payment of the price. Subsequently, as we
saw, the payment became separated from the transfer, so that *mancipatio* represented only the second
element.   The fourth element, that of warranty,
existed to a certain extent in those sales in which
the transfer of property was made by *mancipatio*,
and this fourth element we shall consider further in
a later section.   But throughout the early history of
Rome the first element, indispensable wherever a
sale of any kind takes place, was completely un-

recognised by the law. The reason is that the preliminary agreement between buyer and seller was nothing more than a *pactum*, an agreement without legal force because usually without form. The parties might always of course embody their agreement of sale in a *sponsio* and *restipulatio*, but in such a case all that the law would recognise would be the reciprocal *sponsiones*, not the agreement itself. Why, we may ask, was recognition ever accorded to this preliminary *pactum*? In other words, what was the origin of *emtio uenditio*, which turned the *pactum* into a contract?

Bekker's plausible theory[1] adopted by Muirhead[2] is that contracts of sale were originally entered into by means of reciprocal stipulations, and that the *actio emti* was but a modification of the *actio ex stipulatu* founded on those stipulations, while it borrowed from the *actio ex stipulatu* its characteristic *bonae fidei* clause. But how then did the notion of *bona fides* arise in the *actio ex stipulatu* itself? Bekker seems to have put the cart before the horse, and Mommsen[3] holds the far more reasonable view that the *actio emti* was the original agency by which *bona fides* found its way into the law of contract, in which case the *actio ex stipulatu* must have been not the prototype but the copy of the *actio emti*.

The origin of the *actio emti* was indeed very curious, since it seems clearly to have been suggested and moulded by the influence of public law. The sales of public property, which used at first to be

[1] *Akt.* I. 158.   [2] *Rom. Law*, p. 334.
[3] *Z. der Sav. Stift. R. A.* VI. 265.

carried out by the Consuls and afterwards by the Quaestors[1], became increasingly frequent as the conquests of Rome were multiplied, and as the supplies of booty, slaves and conquered lands became more and more plentiful. The purchase by the State of materials and military supplies was also of frequent occurrence, as the wealth of Rome increased. Now these public *emtiones* and *uenditiones* constantly occurring between private citizens and the State were founded upon agreements necessarily formless. The State could clearly not make a *iusiurandum* or a *sponsio*, but the agreements to which the State was a party (according to the fundamental principle laid down at the beginning of this inquiry that the sanction of publicity was as strong as that of religion) were no less binding than the formal contracts of private law. A public breach of *bona fides* would have been notorious and disgraceful. Whenever therefore the State took part in *emtio uenditio,* the agreement of sale was thereby invested with peculiar solemnity ; and thus in course of time the *pactum uenditionis* became so common as an inviolable contract that the *actio emti uenditi* was created in order to extend the force of the public *emtio uenditio* into the realm of private law. As soon as this action was provided, *emtio uenditio* became a regular contract, which was necessarily bilateral because performance of some sort was required from both parties. An action could thus be brought either by the buyer against a seller who refused to deliver (*actio emti*), or by the

[1] Mommsen, *Z. der Sav. Stift. R. A.* vi. p. 262.

seller against a buyer who failed to pay (*actio uenditi*).

The history of the words *emere uendere* is instructive. We can see that at first they were not strictly correlative. *Vendere* or *uenumdare* meant to sell, not in the sense of agreeing upon a price, but in the sense of transferring in return for money[1]; while *emere* meant originally to take or to receive, without reference to the notion of buying[2]. But neither *emere* nor *uendere* was at first a technical term. *Emere* subsequently got the specialized sense of purchasing for money as distinct from *permutare*, to barter[3], but this particular shade of meaning seems like the *actio* to have had a public origin. The old technical expression for the purchase of goods at public sale was *emtio sub hasta* or *sub corona*, while the object of the sales was to get money for the treasury, and therefore the consideration was naturally paid by purchasers in coin. These public *uenditiones* thus led to three results:

1. The agreement of sale came to the front as the element of chief importance, and as a transaction possessing all the validity of a contract.

2. The word *emere* came to denote the act of buying for money, as distinct from *permutatio* which meant buying in kind.

3. The *uenditio* of public law resting wholly upon consent, which was probably signified by a lifting up of the hand in the act of bidding[4], and being necessarily a transaction *bonae fidei*, it follows that when *emtio*

[1] Voigt, *I. N.* IV. 519.   [2] Paul. Diac. *s. u. emere.*
[3] 21 *Dig.* 1. 19. fr. 5.   [4] Cf. the word *manceps.*

uenditio was made actionable in private law, consent was the only thing required to make the contract perfectly binding, and that the rules applicable to it were those, not of *ius strictum,* but of *bona fides.*

The complete recognition of *emtio uenditio* was only attained by degrees. The first step in that direction seems to have been the granting of an *exceptio rei uenditae et traditae* to a defendant challenged in the possession of a thing which he had honestly obtained by purchase and delivery. The second step was the introduction of the *actio Publiciana,* through which a plaintiff, deprived of the possession of a thing that had been sold and delivered to him (1) by the owner or (2) by one whom he honestly believed to be the owner, might recover it by the fiction of *usucapio*[1].

These remedies, the *exceptio* and the *actio,* were necessary complements to one another. The former was a defensive, the latter an offensive weapon, and they both served to protect a *bona fide* purchaser who had by fair means obtained possession of an object to which in strict law another might lay claim. The *exceptio rei uenditae et traditae*[2] was founded upon an Edict worded somewhat as follows: SI QVIS ID QVOD VENDIDIT ET TRADIDIT NONDVM VSVCAPTVM PETET, EXCEPTIONEM DABO[3]; and in the formula of an action by the seller to recover the thing sold this *exceptio* would have been introduced thus:...*si non eam rem qua de agitur A* *Agerius*

[1] Gai. IV. 36. [2] 44 *Dig.* 1. 20.
[3] Voigt, *I. N.* IV. 517.

N° Negidio vendidit et tradidit......Its effect was to protect the *bona fide* purchaser even of a *res mancipi* against the legal owner who attempted to set up his *dominium ex iure Quiritium.* On the other hand the *actio Publiciana* in its alternative form, was based on two Edicts worded somewhat as follows:

(i) SI QVIS ID QVOD EI TRADITVM EST EX IVSTA CAVSA A DOMINO ET NONDVM VSVCAPTVM PETET, IVDICIVM DABO[1].

(ii) SI QVIS ID QVOD BONA FIDE EMIT ET EI TRADITVM EST NON A DOMINO ET NONDVM VSV-CAPTVM PETET, IVDICIVM DABO[2].

The precise wording of these Edicts is much disputed, but the question of their correct emendation is too large to be discussed here. The formula of an *actio Publiciana* based on the second Edict is given by Gaius[3] and ran as follows: *Si quem hominem A[s] Agerius[4] emit et qui ei traditus est anno possedisset, tum si eum hominem de quo agitur eius ex iure Quiritium esse oporteret, quanti ea res erit, tantam pecuniam, iudex, N[m] Negidium A° Agerio condemnato, s. n. p. a.*

The usefulness of these actions as a protection to sale is apparent. They secured the buyer in possession of the object sold to him until *usucapio* had ripened such possession into full *dominium*; but they were useful only when his possession had been interrupted and he wished to recover it. On the other hand, the *exceptio rei uenditae et traditae* pro-

[1] Voigt, *I. N.* iv. 478.
[2] Voigt, *I. N.* iv. 479.   [3] iv. 36.
[4] *BONA FIDE* here inserted by Voigt, *I. N.* iv. 483, cf. 6 *Dig.* 2. 7. fr. 15.

tected him till the period of *usucapio* against the former owner; but it was only useful where his possession had not been interrupted. The date of the *actio Publiciana* and of this *exceptio* are not to be fixed with absolute certainty; but it is quite clear that neither of them had anything to do with a Praetor Publicius mentioned by Cicero as having existed about A.V.C. 685 [1]. Though there is no mention of either *actio* or *exceptio* in the writers of the Republican period, yet it is clear from some passages of Plautus [2] that the tradition of *res mancipi* sold was in his time a transaction protected by the law, and Voigt [3] has shrewdly argued that both *actio* and *exceptio* must be older than the *actio emti*, because the latter aimed at securing delivery (*habere licere*) which would have been of no use had not delivery already been protected by legal remedies. Now the *Fasti Capitolini* report a Consul M. Publicius Malleolus of A.V.C. 522 [4], and the conjecture that he was the author of the *actio Publiciana* seems very plausible [5]. The *exceptio rei uenditae et traditae* was probably somewhat older, for the defensive would naturally precede, not follow, the offensive remedy. Nor can this *exceptio* in Voigt's opinion have been contemporary with the *actio Publiciana*, because it does not bear the name of *exceptio Publiciana*, which it otherwise would have borne [6]. This argument does not seem to me strong,

[1] Cic. *Cluent.* 45. 126.

[2] *Curc.* 4. 2. 8 ; *Pers.* 4. 3. 64 ; *Epid.* 3. 2. 23.

[3] *I. N.* IV. 469.   [4] = Praetor in A.V.C. 519.

[5] Voigt, *I. N.* IV. 505.   [6] *I. N.* IV. 468.

since we know that the famous *exceptio doli* was not called *exceptio Aquiliana*. But the point is not an important one. It is enough to be able to say with approximate certainty that the *exceptio rei uenditae et traditae* and the *actiones Publicianae* were introduced by some Praetor about A.V.C. 520.

Still the agreement of sale was not yet enforceable as such. In private affairs it remained what it had been from the time of the XII Tables, a formless agreement supported only by the *mores* of the community, whereas in public affairs it was still technically a *pactum* as before, except that the publicity of sales made by the Quaestors gave to their terms a peculiarly binding force. The solemnity always attaching to transactions done in the presence of the people was, as we have seen, at the root of this respect paid to the public *uenditio*.

At last the Praetor of some year decided to make the *emtio uenditio* of private law the ground of an action, and thus put it on a level with the public *uenditiones*. We do not know the terms of the important Edict by which the *actio emti* was introduced, but the formula of the action (*ex uendito*) brought by the seller is partly given by Gaius [1] and must have been as follows : *Quod Aulus Agerius mensam N^o Negidio uendidit, quidquid paret ob eam rem N^m Negidium A^o Agerio dare facere oportere ex fide bona* [2], *eius, iudex, N^m Negidium A^o Agerio condemnato. s. n. p. a.* The *intentio* here was exactly the same as that of the *actio ex stipulatu*, and was probably its prototype, both of them being equally

[1] IV. 131.   [2] Cic. *Off.* III. 16. 66.

bonae fidei actions.   The formula of the action (*ex emto*) brought by the purchaser was worded in like fashion: *Quod A[s] Agerius de N[o] Negidio hominem quo de agitur emit, quidquid ob eam rem N[m] Negidium A[o] Agerio dare facere oportet ex fide bona, eius, iudex, &c. &c.*

The age of the *actio emti* has been very hotly disputed, and the most knotty question has been whether the action existed or not in the days of Plautus, who died A.V.C. 570. The chief opponent of the affirmative theory has been Bekker[1], but the arguments of Demelius[2], Costa[3], Voigt[4] and Bechmann[5] are so convincing that little doubt on the subject can any longer be entertained. It appears absolutely certain that the *actio emti* was a feature of the law as Plautus knew it. An elaborate proof of this proposition has been so well given by Demelius and Costa that it is not necessary to do more than sum up the evidence.

(i)   The contract of *emtio uenditio* was discussed by Sex. Aelius Paetus Catus (Cos. A.V.C. 556) probably in his *Tripertita,* and by C. Liuius Drusus (Cos. A.V.C. 642)[6].

(ii)   The aedilician Edict, which presupposed that *emtio uenditio* was actionable, is mentioned by Plautus[7].

(iii)   We find in Plautus many passages which are only intelligible on the supposition that *emtio*

[1] *Akt.* I. 146, note 38.
[2] *Z. für RG.* II. 177.
[3] *Dir. Privato* 365–73.
[4] *I. N.* IV. 542.
[5] *Kauf,* I. pp. 511–526.
[6] 19 *Dig.* 1. 38.
[7] *Capt.* 4. 2. 43.

uenditio was actionable. For instance in *Mostellaria*[1], where the son of Theuropides pretends. to have bought a house, and where the owner of the house is represented as begging for a rescission of the sale, we cannot suppose, as Bekker does[2], that *fides* was the only thing which bound the owner. Had it not been for the existence of the *actio emti* he could not have been represented as trying to have the sale cancelled[3].

Again, in Act 5, Scene 1, the slave Tranio advises his master Theuropides to call the owner into court and bring an action for the mancipation of the house[4], and this can be nothing else than a reference to the *actio ex emto*. In the same play[5] it is also plain that *bona fides* was a principle controlling the *iudicium ex emto*.

Again in *Persa*[6] it is clear that Sagaristio, when selling the slave-girl, would not have taken such pains to disclaim all warranty if he could not have been compelled by the *actio emti* to make good the loss sustained by the purchaser. To prevent this liability Sagaristio is careful to throw the whole *periculum* on the buyer. Why should he have done so, had there been no *actio emti* ?

Again in *Rudens* the *leno*, who had taken earnest-money for the sale of a slave girl and had then absconded with her, would not have been so much afraid of meeting the buyer Plesidippus, if he

---

[1] 3. 1. and 2.   [2] *de Empt. Vend.* p. 16.
[3] 3. 2. 110.
[4] 5. 1. 43. Cf. Gai. IV. 131.   [5] 3. 1. 139.
[6] 4. 4. 114. and 4. 7. 5.

had not feared the *actio emti*. And when the slave girl was finally *abiudicata* from the *leno*[1], Demelius and Costa are unquestionably right in regarding this as a result of a *iudicium ex emto*. Bekker's opinion that it was the result of a *uindicatio in libertatem* seems hardly to agree with the fact that the *leno* is not represented as knowing of her free status till two scenes later[2]. We might multiply instances, but the evidence is so fully given by others that it is not worth repeating. The general conclusion to be drawn from the above facts is that *emtio uenditio* became actionable before A.V.C. 550; and, if our argument be right, later than 520, the date of the *actio Publiciana*.

From Plautus we gather further that *arrha* or *arrhabo*, the pledge or earnest money which Gaius mentions in this connection, was often given to bind the bargain of sale as well as other bargains. From this it has been argued that pure *consensus* must have been insufficient to make the contract binding[3]; but, if that be so, why should the *arrha* have been used in Gaius' day, when we know that sale was purely consensual? In *Rudens*[4] it is clear that the *arrhabo* was not a necessary part of the transaction, but a mere piece of evidence, so that *arrhabonem acceperat* simply means *uendiderat*[5]. The use of *arrhabo* is mentioned also in *Mostellaria*[6] and *Poenulus*[7]. It was probably forfeited by the purchaser in case the bargain fell through.

[1] 5. 1. 1.   [2] 5. 3—8.
[3] Bekker, *Heid. Krit. Jahrschrift*, I. 444.
[4] 2. 6. 70.   [5] *Rud. Prol.* 45–6.
[6] 3. 1. 111—4. 4. 21.   [7] 5. 6. 22.

Having now seen how the *actio emti uenditi* originated and what was its probable age, let us see what obligations were imposed by the conclusion of the sale upon each of the parties to it:

(1) Upon the purchaser (*emtor*).

His chief duty was *reddere pretium*, to pay the price agreed upon [1], and if the price consisted partly of things in kind, his duty was to deliver them [2]; but according to Voigt [3] there was no obligation upon him to do more than deliver.

A duty which the purchaser seems very early to have acquired was that of compensating the seller for *mora* on his part [4].

(2) Upon the vendor (*uenditor*).

His chief duty was *rem praestare* [5] (or *rem habere licere*), to give quiet possession to the vendee; but this did not include the obligation to convey *dominium ex iure Quiritium* [6].

The *actio emti*, as we have now examined it, enforced three things: (1) recognition of the consensual agreement of sale, (2) delivery by the seller, (3) prompt payment by the buyer. Thus it dealt with three of the elements involved in the general conception of sale. The fourth element, that of warranty, remains to be considered.

We know that this fourth element was covered by the *actio emti* in the time of Ulpian, but it does not seem to have been so during the Republic. Both Muirhead [7] and Bechmann [8] have involved the

---

[1] Varro, *R. R.* II. 2. 6. [2] Cato, *R. R.* 150.
[3] *I. N.* III. 985. [4] 19 *Dig.* 1. 38 fr. 1.
[5] 19 *Dig.* 1. 11. [6] 19 *Dig.* 1. 30; 18 *Dig.* 1. 25.
[7] *R. Law*, p. 285. [8] *Kauf.* I. 505.

subject in unnecessary difficulty by confusing a *bonae fidei* contract of sale with one in which warranty was employed. They speak as though *bona fides* included warranty, a proposition not necessarily true and of which we have no proof. It appears, on the contrary, that the *actio emti* to enforce warranty was of much later origin than the *actio emti* to enforce consensual sale [1]. We have therefore to inquire how warranty was originally given and how it was made good.

The only kind of warranty which we have hitherto encountered is that against eviction implied in every *mancipatio* and enforced by the *actio auctoritatis*. This method was but of limited scope, since it applied only to *res mancipi*.

After the introduction of the *condictio incerti*, it became possible to embody warranties in the form of a stipulation. This was accomplished in one or more of the following ways:

(1) The *stipulatio duplae* specified the warranty given by the vendor, and provided in case of a breach for liquidated damages in the shape of a *poena dupli*, which was doubtless copied from the *duplum* of the *actio auctoritatis*. The best specimens of this stipulation are texts 1 and 2 of the Transylvanian Tablets printed by Bruns [2]. It was apparently used in those sales of *res mancipi*, which were consummated not by *mancipatio* but by *traditio* [3]. Its superiority to the warranty afforded by the *actio auctoritatis* was that it guaranteed quality as well as title, which the *actio*

---

[1] Girard, *Stip. de Garantie, N. R. H. de D.* VII. p. 545 note.
[2] *Font.* p. 256.   [3] Varro, *R. R.* II. 10. 5.

auctoritatis could not do. The Tablets indeed show that the warranties against defects in this stipulation were exceedingly comprehensive, and that it defended against eviction not only the buyer, but also those in privity with him (*emtorem eumue ad quem ea res pertinebit*).

(2) We also find a *stipulatio simplae*, of which the best instances are texts 3 and 4 of the Transylvanian Tablets and which, according to Varro [1], might be used as an alternative to the *stipulatio duplae*, if preferred by the two parties. Its aim in securing the buyer against eviction and defects was precisely the same as that of the former stipulation; its only difference being that the damages were but half the former amount, i.e. were exactly measured by the price of the thing sold. Girard and Voigt are probably wrong in identifying this stipulation used for *res mancipi* with the next one, which was apparently used only in sales of *res nec mancipi*.

(3) Another stipulation of frequent occurrence was the stipulation *recte habere licere*. This guaranteed quiet possession so far as the seller was concerned. Its scope was therefore not so wide as that of the *stipulatio simplae* or *duplae*. The vendor simply promised *recte habere licere*, but specified no penalty in the event of his non-performance, so that the action on the stipulation must have been a *condictio incerti*, in which the damages were assessed by the judge. The import of the word '*recte*' was doubtless not the same as that of *ex fide bona*; but,

[1] *R. R.* II. 2. 5.

as Bechmann[1] has pointed out, it simply implied a waiver of technical objections.

(4) A stipulation as to quality alone is mentioned by Varro[2] as annexed to the sale of oxen and other *res mancipi.* The vendor simply promised *sanos praestari,* so that in this case also the remedy was *condictio incerti* for judicial damages.

(5) A *satisdatio secundum mancipium* is also mentioned by Cicero[3] and in the Baetic Tablet[4]. But its nature and form are quite uncertain. Its name implies that it had some connection with *auctoritas,* and the most likely theory seems to be that it was a stipulation of suretyship, by which security was given for the *auctor,* either to insure his appearance (and if so, it was a form of *uadimonium*[5]) or to guarantee his payment of the *poena dupli,* in the event of eviction (and if so, it was a form of *fideiussio*[6]).

The three first of the above stipulations prove that even in the early Empire (A.D. 160 is the supposed date of the Transylvanian Tablets) *actio emti* was not yet an action for implied warranty. Ulpian's language also indicates that the implication of warranty was a new doctrine in his day[7].

Thus far we have seen that stipulations of warranty were customary, and that by the *stipulatio duplae* or *simplae* both title and quality were secured. The next step was to make these stipu-

[1] *Kauf.* I. p. 639.
[2] II. 5. 11.
[3] *ad Att.* v. 1. 2.
[4] Bruns, *Fontes,* p. 251.
[5] Varro, VI. 7. 54.
[6] See Girard, *loc. cit.* p. 551.
[7] 21 *Dig.* 1. 31 fr. 20.

lations compulsory, and this was first accomplished
by the Aediles, in their Edict regulating, among
other things, sales in the open market. Plautus
mentions this Edict, and refers to the rule of *red-
hibitio* which it enforced[1]. The first positive mention
of aedilician regulations as to warranty occurs however in Cicero[2], and from this it appears that the
Aediles first compelled a *stipulatio duplae* in the sale
of slaves. This innovation was doubtless intended to
punish slave dealers, who were, as Plautus shows, a
low and dishonest class, by imposing upon them the
old penalty of *duplum.* The two aedilician actions
which could be brought, if the *stipulatio duplae* had
not been given, were (1) the *actio redhibitoria*, available within two months, and by which the vendor
had to restore the *duplum* of the price[3]; (2) the
actio quanti emtoris intersit[4], available within six
months for simple damages. Further than this,
however, the law of the Republic did not advance.
It was not till the day of Trajan and Septimius
Severus that the stipulations of warranty were
compulsory for other things than slaves[5], and we
cannot therefore here trace the development of
warranty to its consummation.

Art. 2. LOCATIO CONDVCTIO. The word *locare*
has no technical equivalent in English, for it sometimes expresses the fact of hiring, sometimes that of
being hired. It means literally to place, to put out.

[1] *Capt.* 4. 2. 44; *Rud.* 2. 3. 42; *Most.* 3. 2. 113.
[2] *Off.* III. 17. 71.
[3] 21 *Dig.* 1. 45.　　　　[4] 21 *Dig.* 1. 28.
[5] Girard, *N. R. H. de D.* VIII. p. 425.

As we say that a capitalist places his money, so the Romans said of him *pecunias locat*[1]. The State was said *opus locare* when it paid a contractor for doing a job, while the gladiator who got paid for fighting was said *operas locare*. This contract was consensual and bi-lateral like *emtio uenditio,* and had a very similar origin. It is easy indeed to see that for a long time there was no distinction made between *locatio* and *uenditio*. The latter meant originally, as we have seen, to transfer for a consideration, and thus included the hire as well as the sale of an object. Festus accordingly says that the *locationes* made by the Censors were originally called *uenditiones*[2]. The confusion thus produced left its traces deeply imprinted in the later law, for we find Gaius' remarks on *locatio conductio* chiefly devoted to a discussion of how in certain doubtful cases the line should be drawn between that and *emtio uenditio*.

Like *emtio uenditio*, this contract was developed in connection with the administration of public business. The public affairs in which contractual relations necessarily arose were of four kinds[3]:

(1) Sales of public property, such as land, slaves, etc., which devolved upon the Quaestors. This class of transactions produced the contract of *emtio uenditio,* as above explained.

(2) Contracts for the hire of public servants, generally known as *apparitores*. These were the *lictores* and other attendants upon the different

---

[1] *Most.* 1. 3. 85.   [2] Festus, s. u. *uenditiones.*
[3] Mommsen, *Z. der Sav. Stif. R. A.* vi. 262.

magistrates, and were naturally engaged by those whom they respectively served. This hiring gave rise to the contract known as *conductio operarum*, while the offer of such services to the State constituted *locatio operarum*.

(3) Business agreements connected with public work, such as the building of temples or bridges, the collection of revenue, etc. This class was in charge of the Censors[1], and developed the contract of *locatio operis*, while the transaction viewed from the standpoint of the contractor became known as *conductio operis*.

(4) Agreements for the supply of various kinds of necessaries for the service of the State, such as beasts of burden, waggons, provisions, etc. This hiring produced the contract known as *conductio rei*, while the contractors who supplied such commodities were said *rem locare*.

Thus the first group of public transactions gave birth to the contract of sale in private law, while the three last groups each became the parent of one of the three forms of the contract of hire.

Just as *uenditio* seems to have been the original equivalent of *locatio*, so must *emtio* have been the original term for what was afterwards known as *conductio*. *Conducere* can originally have applied only to the second class of agreements; it must have denoted the collecting and bringing together of a body of *apparitores*. Afterwards, when the notion of hiring became conspicuous, *conducere* doubtless lost its narrow meaning, and was extended to

[1] Liu. XLII. 3.

the other two kinds of hire, as the correlative to *locare* [1].

The wholly distinct origin of these various kinds of *locatio conductio,* and the fact that they were transacted by different magistrates, are sufficient reasons for the curious distinction which the classical jurisprudence always drew between *locatio conductio rei, operis* and *operarum.* A trace of the old word *emere* as equivalent to *conducere* always remained in the word *redemtor,* meaning a contractor for public works. This term was never applied to the *apparitor,* since it was he who took the initiative and who was thence regarded as a *locator operarum.*

When the conception of *locatio conductio* became separated from that of *emtio uenditio* it is impossible to determine. But since the two transactions appear in Plautus distinct as well as enforceable, and since the contract of sale was only recognised shortly before Plautus' day, the conceptions of sale and of hire probably became quite distinct before either transaction became actionable. We can trace in many passages of Plautus the three forms *locatio rei* [2], *locatio operis* [3], *locatio operarum* [4]; and it can hardly be imagined that these contracts could have been so common and so distinctly marked had they not been provided with actions. Voigt [5] however is of opinion that the three different forms of *locatio conductio* became actionable at different periods. *Locatio conductio*

[1] Mommsen, *ib.* p. 266.
[2] *Pseud.* 4. 7. 90 ; *Merc.* 3. 2. 17.
[3] *Bacch.* 4. 3. 115 ; *Persa,* 1. 3. 80.
[4] *Aul.* 2. 4. 1 ; *Merc.* 3. 4. 78 ; *Epid.* 2. 3. 8.
[5] *I. N.* iv. 596, ff.

operis and *operarum* he places earliest, and admits
that they were known as contracts by the middle of
the sixth century, which would bring them very
nearly to the age of *emtio uenditio*; but from
Cato[1] he infers that *locatio conductio rei* was of later
origin and that it did not become actionable until
the first half of the seventh century. The earliest
actual mention that we possess of *locatio conductio* is
by Quintus Mucius Scaeuola, author of 18 books on
the *Ius Ciuile*[2], whom Cicero quotes[3], though we
cannot tell whether the quotation refers to all
kinds of *locatio conductio* or only to the *locatio
conductio operis*. Certain it is that in Cato[4] *locatio
conductio rei* seems to be treated rather as *emtio
uenditio fructus rei*. It is also remarkable that *locatio conductio rei* is seldom mentioned in Plautus[5],
and so briefly that we can form no conclusion as to
whether it was or was not actionable; whereas on
the contrary *locatio conductio operis* and *operarum*
appear very often and exhibit all the marks of
thoroughly developed contracts. For instance, the
locatio conductio operarum in *Asinaria*[6] contains a
lex commissoria, and that in *Bacchides*[7] provides for a
bond to be given by the *locator operarum* binding
him to release the person whose *operae* he had been
employing, as soon as the work was finished. Again
in *Miles Gloriosus*[8] the technical term *improbare
opus* is used to express the rejection of work badly
carried out by a contractor. All this points to the

[1] *R. R.* 149.   [2] A.V.C. 661–672.   [3] *Off.* III. 17. 70.
[4] *R. R.* 149, 150.   [5] *Curc.* 4. 1. 3; *Merc.* 3. 2. 17.
[6] 1. 3. 76.   [7] 1. 1. 8.   [8] 4. 4. 37.

existence of an action for *locatio conductio operarum*
and for *locatio conductio operis* at the time when
Plautus wrote[1]; but Voigt seems right in concluding
that *locatio conductio rei* did not become actionable
till a good deal later.

The origin of this action, as of the *actio emti*, was
in the Praetor's Edict[2], and in form it differed but
little from the *actio emti uenditi*. Like the latter it
was *bonae fidei*[3] and its form (*ex locato*) must have
been as follows: *Quod A[s] Agerius N[o] Negidio
operas locauit, quidquid paret ob eam rem N[m] Negidium A[o] Agerio dare facere oportere ex fide bona,
eius, iudex, N[m] Negidium A[o] Agerio condemnato.
s. n. p. a.* Like *emtio uenditio* it is also clear that
locatio conductio of all kinds could be made by mere
consensus, and that from the first it must have been
a *bonae fidei* contract like its prototype.

The writings of Cato[4] are our chief authority for
the existence of the *locatio conductio operis* and
operarum in the second half of the seventh century,
and for the manner in which these *locationes* were
contracted. It appears to have been customary to
draw up with care the terms (*leges locationis*) of such
contracts, and when these were committed to writing,
as they doubtless must have been, they exactly
corresponded to the contracts made in modern
times between employers and contractors.

Already in the Republican period the jurists had

---

[1] So Demelius, *Z. für RG.* II. 193 ; Bechmann, *Kauf.* I. p. 526 ;
but Bekker denies it *Z. für RG.* III. 442.

[2] 50 *Dig.* 16. 5.   [3] Cic. *N. D.* III. 30. 74 ; *Off.* II. 18. 64.
[4] *R. R.* 141–5.

begun to subdivide the classes of contracts above mentioned.

(1)   They distinguished between various sorts of *locatio conductio rei*.   There was (*a*) *rei locatio fruendae* in which the use of the object was granted[1], (*b*) *rei locatio ut eadem reddatur* in which the object itself had to be returned, and (*c*) *rei locatio ut eiusdem generis reddatur*[2] in which a thing of the same kind might be returned.

(2)   The two kinds of *locatio conductio operis* were also most probably distinguished at an early date into: (*a*) *locatio rei faciendae* in which a thing was given out to be made (ἔργον), and (*b*) *locatio operis faciendi*[3] in which a job was given out to be done (ἀποτέλεσμα).

(3)   *Locatio conductio operarum* alone does not seem to have been subdivided in any way.

The object of these distinctions was doubtless to define in each case the rights and duties of the *conductor*.   The technical expression for the remuneration in *locatio conductio* was *merx*[4], and it was always a sum of money, probably because it was originally paid out of the *aerarium* and therefore could not conveniently have been given in kind. The fact that in Plautus the word *pretium* was often used instead of *merx*, shows that the distinction between *locatio conductio* and *emtio uenditio* was still of recent origin when he wrote; but our general conclusion must be that this contract was known

---

[1] Gai. III. 145 ; *Lex agraria*, c. 25.

[2] 19 *Dig.* 2. 31 ; 34 *Dig.* 2. 34.

[3] 19 *Dig.* 2. 30 ; 50 Dig. 16. 5.   [4] Varro, *L. L.* v. 36.

to him in some at least of its forms, and that in all its branches it arrived at full maturity in the Republican period.

It is worth remembering that the *Lex Rhodia de iactu,* the parent of the modern law of general average, was enforced by means of this action. The owner sued the ship's *magister ex locato,* and the *magister* forced other owners to contribute by suing them *ex conducto*[1]. This law was discussed in Republican times by Servius Sulpicius and Ofilius[2].

Art. 3. Before proceeding further with our history of the *ius gentium* contracts we must notice the important innovation made by the Edict *Pacta conuenta,* the author of which was C. Cassius Longinus, Praetor A. V. C. 627[3]. We have seen how the *pactum uenditionis* and the *pactum locationis* had been recognised and transformed into regular contracts about seventy years before this time. The present Edict gave legal recognition to *pacta* in general, and thus rendered immense assistance in the development of formless Contract.

Its language was somewhat as follows[4]: PACTA CONVENTA, QVAE NEC VI NEC DOLO MALO NEC ADVERSVS LEGES PLEBISCITA EDICTA MAGISTRATVVM FACTA ERVNT, SERVABO.

The scope of the Edict was, however, less broad than might at first be supposed. It might well be understood to mean that *all* lawful agreements would thenceforth be judicially enforceable. But as a matter of fact the test of what should constitute

[1] Carnazzà, *Dir. Com.* p. 172.   [2] 14 *Dig.* 2. 2. fr. 3.
[3] Voigt, *Röm. RG.* i. 591.   [4] 2 *Dig.* 14. 7. fr. 7.

an enforceable *pactum* lay in the discretion of the individual Praetor. He might or might not grant an action, according as the particular agreement set up by the plaintiff did or did not appear to him a valid one. This Edict was therefore nothing more than an official announcement that the Praetor would, in proper cases, give effect to *pacta* which had never before been the objects of judicial cognizance. It needs no explanation to show what important results such an Edict was sure to produce, even in the hands of the most conservative Praetors; and accordingly we find that in the next century new varieties of formless contract arose from the habitual enforcement by the Praetor of corresponding *pacta*.

The mode in which tentative recognition was accorded to the new praetorian *pacta* was the devising of an *actio in factum*[1] to suit each new set of circumstances. The formula of such an action simply set forth the agreement, and directed the judge to assess damages if he should find it to have been broken. This was doubtless the means by which *societas, mandatum, depositum, commodatum, pignus, hypotheca, receptum, constitutum*—in short, all the contractual relations originating in the last century of the Republic—were at first protected and enforced. A curious historical parallel might be drawn between these *actiones in factum* and our "actions on the case." Not only are the terms almost synonymous, but the adaptability of each class of actions to new circumstances was equally remarkable; and the part played by the

[1] 2 *Dig.* 14. 7. fr. 2.

latter class in the expansion of the English Law of
Tort bears a striking resemblance to that played
by the former in the development of the Roman
Law of Contract.

We shall see specimens of the *actio in factum*
based upon the edict *Pacta conuenta*, when we come
to examine the various contracts of the later Republic which all owed their origin to the Praetor's
Edict.

Art. 4. MANDATVM. The age of the *actio mandati* is difficult to fix, but there are good reasons for
believing that it was the third *bonae fidei* action
devised by the Praetor, and that it is older than
the *actio pro socio. Mandatum* was an agreement
whereby one person, at the request of another,
usually his friend[1], undertook the gratuitous performance of something to the interest of that other[2].
In short, it was a special agency in which the agent
received no remuneration. Its gratuitous character
was essential, for where the agent was paid, the
transaction was regarded as a case of *locatio conductio.*
We know that the *testamentum per aes et libram* was
virtually a *mandatum* to the *familiae emtor*[3], and
that *fideicommissa,* which began to be important
towards the end of the Republic, were nothing but
mandata[4]; it is plain too that as an informal transaction *mandatum* must always have been practised
long before it became recognised by the Praetor.

The earliest piece of direct evidence[5] which we

[1] Cic. *Rosc. Am.* 39. 112.   [2] Gai. III. 156.
[3] Gai. II. 102.   [4] Ulp. *Frag.* 25. 1–3.
[5] Auct. ad Her. II. 13. 19.

have as to the *actio mandati* is that it existed in
A.V.C. 631 under the Praetorship of S. Iulius Caesar.
It is probable that the action was then of recent
origin, and represented the first-fruits of the Edict
Pacta conuenta[1], for Caesar treated it as non-
hereditary, whereas the Praetor Marcus Drusus soon
afterwards granted an *actio in heredem* according to
the rule of the later law[2].

From Plautus it distinctly appears that *mandatum*
was a well developed institution in his day, but there
is no evidence to prove that an *actio mandati* already
existed. The transaction is often mentioned[3], and
must have been necessary in the active commercial
life which Plautus has pourtrayed. In *Trinummus*[4],
for instance, we see a regular case of *mandatum
generale*. The phrase "*mandare fidei et fiduciae*"
here indicates that *fides* pure and simple was the
only support on which *mandatum* rested, and that
there was no motive beyond friendly feeling to
compel the performance of the *mandatum*. On the
other hand the word *infamia* is thought to have had
a technical meaning, as an allusion to the fact that
the *actio mandati* was *famosa*[5]; but this is surely
a flimsy basis for Demelius' opinion that the *actio
mandati* was in existence as early as the middle of
the sixth century[6].

It seems much safer to regard this action as

[1] Voigt, *Röm. RG.* I. 681.   [2] 17 Dig. 1. 58.

[3] E.g. *Bacch.* 3. 3. 71–5; *Capt.* 2. 2. 93; *Asin.* 1. 1. 107;
Epid. 1. 2. 27, 31; *Cist.* 4. 2. 53.

[4] 1. 2. 72–121.

[5] Cic. *pro S. Rosc.* 38. 111; *Caec.* 3. 7.

[6] *Z. für RG.* II. 198; Costa, *Dir. Priv.* p. 390.

younger than those of *emtio uenditio* and *locatio
conductio,* and to trace its origin to the influence of
the Edict *Pacta conuenta.* The earliest form of
relief granted to the agent against his *mandator* was
doubtless an *actio in factum,* based upon that Edict,
and having a formula of this kind[1]:

*Si paret N^m Negidium A^o Agerio, cum is in
potestate L^i Titii esset, mandauisse ut pro se solueret,
et A^m Agerium emancipatum soluisse, quanti ea res
erit, tantam pecuniam iudex N^m Negidium A^o Agerio
condemna. s. n. p. a.*

When at length the Praetor was prepared to
recognise *mandatum* as a regular contract of the *ius
ciuile,* he placed it on an equal footing with the older
bonae fidei contracts by granting the *actio mandati,*
with its far more flexible *formula in ius concepta.*
The *actio mandati directa* brought by the principal
against the agent had the following formula :

*Quod A^s Agerius N^o Negidio rem curandam man-
dauit, quidquid paret ob eam rem N^m Negidium A^o
Agerio dare facere praestare oportere ex fide bona, eius,
iudex, N^m Negidium A^o Agerio condemna. s. n. p. a.*

In the *actio contraria,* by which the agent sued
the principal, the formula began as above, but the
condemnatio was different, thus:

*......quidquid paret ob eam rem A^m Agerium N^o
Negidio dare facere praestare oportere e. f. b. eius
A^m Agerium N^o Negidio condemna. s. n. p. a.*

Or again, where the claims and counter-claims
were conflicting, the *condemnatio* might be made
still more indefinite, thus:

[1] 17 *Dig.* 1. 12. fr. 6.

...... *quidquid paret ob eam rem alterum alteri dare facere praestare oportere e. f. b. eius alterum alteri condemna. s. n. p. a.*[1]

Unfortunately we do not know the language of the Edict by which the *actio mandati* was instituted; but the fact that it was modelled on the actions of sale and hire is one that nobody disputes.

There is no direct authority for assuming the existence of an *actio in factum* in this case, as there is in the cases of *commodatum* and *depositum*, where we have Gaius' express statement to that effect[2]. But it is clear, from Gaius' allusion to "*quaedam causae*" and from his use of "*uelut*," that double formulae existed in many other actions. We may well accept Lenel's ingenious theory[3] that the existence of an *actio contraria* always indicates the existence of formulae *in ius* and *in factum conceptae,* and the assumption here made is therefore no rash conjecture.

The conception of *mandatum* changed somewhat before the end of the Republic. It meant at first any charge general or special[4]. But by Cicero's time it had acquired the narrow meaning, which it retained throughout the classical period, of a particular trust[5], while *procuratio* was used of a general trust[6], and its remedy was the *actio negotiorum gestorum*[7].

Thus it still remains for us to inquire to what

---

[1] Lenel, *Ed. Perp.* p. 235.

[2] Gai. IV. 47.

[3] *Ed. Perp.* p. 202.

[4] Cato, *R. R.* 141–3.

[5] 17 *Dig.* 1. 48.

[6] Cic. *Top.* 10. 42.

[7] Gai. in 3 *Dig.* 3. 46.

extent *procuratio,* i.e. general agency, was practised, as distinguished from *mandatum generale,* i.e. special agency with general instructions, and how general agents (*procuratores*) were appointed.

Now it is one of the most striking features of the Roman Law that agency of this sort was unknown until almost the end of the Republic. How and why so great a commercial people as the Romans managed to do without agency, is a question that has received many different answers. We may be sure that *mandatum* was practised long before it ever became actionable, but if so, it was practised informally and had no legal recognition. The circumstance which made it almost impossible for general agency to exist was that the Romans held fast to the rigid rule: "*id quod nostrum est sine facto nostro ad alium transferri non potest*[1]." Such a rule evidently had its origin in the early period when contracts were strictly formal, and when he alone who uttered the solemn words or who touched the scales was capable of acquiring rights. In a formal period the rule was natural enough; but the curious thing is that it should not have been relaxed as soon as the real and consensual contracts became important.

This fact has sometimes been accounted for on ethical grounds. It has been said that the keen legal conscience of the Romans made them loth to depart from the letter of the law by admitting that a man who entered into a contract could possibly thereby acquire anything for anybody else. But the true

[1] 50 *Dig.* 17. 11.

reason seems rather to have been a practical one [1]—
that the existence of an agency of status precluded
that of an agency of contract. Thus we know that
householders as a rule had sons or slaves who could
receive promises by stipulation, though they could
not bind their *paterfamilias* by a disadvantageous
contract; and so to a limited extent agency always
existed within the Roman family. It is also obvious
that, in an age when men seldom went on long
journeys, the necessity for an agent or fully empowered representative cannot have been seriously
felt. Plautus shows however that agency was not
developed even in his day, when travel had become
comparatively common. In *Trinummus* and *Mostellaria*, for instance, no prudent friend is charged with
the affairs of the absent father, and consequently the
spendthrift son makes away with his father's goods
by lending or selling them as he pleases [2].

We can however mark the various stages by
which the Roman Law approximated more and
more closely to the idea of true agency.

1. The oldest class of general agents were the
tutores to whom belonged the management (*gestio*)
of a ward's or woman's affairs, and the *curatores* of
young men and of the insane.

2. The next oldest kind of general agents were
the *cognitores*, persons appointed to conduct a particular piece of litigation [3], and not to be confounded
with the *cognitores* of *praediatura* [4]. They were ori-

---

[1] Pernice, *Labeo*, I. 489.   [2] *Trin.* 1. 2. 129; *Most.* 1. 1. 74.

[3] 2 *Verr.* III. 60. 137 ; *Caec.* 14.

[4] *Lex. Malac.* 63 ; Cic. *Har. Resp.* 45.

ginally appointed only in cases of age or illness[1], and their general authority was limited to the management of the given suit. Gaius has shown us how they were able to conduct an action by having their names inserted in the *condemnatio*[2]. Whether they existed or not under the *legis actio* procedure is uncertain; but they probably did, since we know that they were at first appointed in a formal manner[3]. Subsequently the Edict extended their powers to the informally appointed *procuratores*. The action by which these agents were made responsible to their principals was after Labeo's time the *actio mandati*[4]. During the Republic however and before his time the jurists do not seem to have regarded the relation between *cognitor* and principal as a case of *mandatum*, but simply gave an action corresponding to each particular case, as for instance an *actio depositi* if the *cognitor* failed to restore a *depositum.*

3. *Procuratores* were persons who in Cicero's day[5] acted as the agents and representatives of persons absent on public business[6]. They often appear to have been[7] the freedmen of their respective principals, and their functions were doubtless modelled on those of the *curatores*. The connection between *curatores* and *procuratores* is seen in the Digest where *pupilli* and absent individuals are often coupled together[8], while the

[1] Auct. ad Her. ii. 20.   [2] Gai. iv. 86.
[3] Gai. iv. 83.   [4] 17 *Dig*. 1. 8. fr. 1.
[5] *Quint*. 19. 60–62; 2 *Verr*. v. 7. 15; *Lex Iul. Mun*. 1.
[6] *Caec*. 57.   [7] Cic. *Or*. 2. 249.
[8] 29 *Dig*. 7. 2. fr. 3; 47 *Dig*. 10. 17. fr. 11; 50 *Dig*. 17. 124.

definitions of *procurator* show that his power was
confined to occasions on which his principal was
absent[1], and the word *procuratio* itself indicates
that it was copied from the *curatio* of *furiosi*[2] or of
prodigi.

One passage of Gaius[3] seems to imply that the
procurator was not always carefully distinguished
from the *negotiorum gestor* or voluntary agent, and
Pernice interprets some remarks of Cicero[4] as indi-
cating the same fact. From this he infers with much
likelihood[5] that the remedy against the *procurator*
was originally not the *actio mandati* but the *actio
negotiorum gestorum*[6]. Even in Labeo's time the
actio mandati was probably not well established in
the case of *procuratores*, though it was so by the
time of Gaius[7].

A *procurator* might conduct litigation for the
absent principal[8]; but the acquisition of property
through an agent was not clearly established even
in Cicero's time[9], though the principal could always
bring an action for the profits of a contract made
in his name[10].

4. *Negotiorum gestio* was a relation not based
upon contract, but consisted in the voluntary intervention of a self-appointed agent, who undertook
to administer the affairs of some absent or deceased
friend. In the Institutes it is classed as a form of

---

[1] Paul. Diac. *s.u. cognitor.*   [2] *Lex agr.* c. 69.
[3] IV. 84.   [4] *Top.* 42 and 66.   [5] 17 *Dig.* 1. 6. fr. 1.
[6] *Labeo*, I. 494.   [7] 4 *Dig.* 4. 25. fr. 1.
[8] 3 *Dig.* 3. 33.   [9] Cic. *Att.* VI. 1. 4.
[10] 3 *Dig.* 3. 46. fr. 4.

quasi-contract, and it was always regarded as a relation closely analogous to *mandatum*[1].

The mode of enforcing claims made by the *negotiorum gestor* and his principal against one another was the *actio negotiorum gestorum*, which might, like the *actio mandati*, be either *directa* or *contraria*. It was based upon an Edict worded thus:

SI QVIS NEGOTIA ALTERIVS, SIVE QVIS NEGOTIA QVAE CVIVSQVE CVM IS MORITVR FVERINT, GESSERIT, IVDICIVM EO NOMINE DABO[2].

We do not know the date of this Edict, but it was certainly issued before the end of the Republic, inasmuch as the action founded upon it was discussed by Trebatius and Ofilius[3]. This action had a formula *in ius concepta* which ran somewhat as follows:

Quod N[s] Negidius negotia A[i] Agerii gessit, qua de re agitur, quidquid ob eam rem N[m] Negidium A[o] Agerio dare facere praestare oportet ex fide bona, tantam pecuniam iudex N[m] Negidium A[o] Agerio condemna. s. n. p. a.[4]

5. Another means by which agency could practically be brought about was *adstipulatio*, as we saw above[5]. This was not a case of true agency, for the *adstipulator* acquired the claim in his own name, and if he sued upon it, he did so of course in his own right: yet he was treated as agent for the other *stipulator* and made liable to the *actio mandati*[6].

6. *Fideiussio* was probably treated as a form of special agency almost from the time of its invention,

[1] 3 *Dig.* 5. 18. fr. 2.	[2] 3 *Dig.* 5. 3.
[3] 17 *Dig.* 1. 22. fr. 10.	[4] Lenel, *Ed. Perp.* p. 86.
[5] p. 110.	[6] Gai. III. 111.

since we know that it possessed the remedy of the
actio mandati as early as the time of Quintus Mucius
Scaeuola [1].

Art. 5.   SOCIETAS.   This was the common name
given to several kinds of contract by which two or
more persons might combine together for a common
profitable purpose to which they contributed the
necessary means.   These contracts could be formed
by mere consent of the parties, and except in the
case of *societas uectigalis* they were dissolved by the
death of any one member, so that even *societas in
perpetuum* meant only an association for so long as
the parties should live [2].

Ulpian distinguishes four kinds of *societas* [3]: (1)
omnium bonorum, (2) *negotiationis alicuius*, (3) *rei
unius*, and (4) *uectigalis*.

The first of these has no counterpart in our
modern law, but may be described as a contractual
tenancy in common.   The second and third may be
treated under one head, as *societates quaestuariae*,
corresponding to modern contracts of partnership.
The fourth may best be regarded as the Roman
equivalent of the modern corporation.

Except in the case of this fourth form, which
was in most respects unique, the remedy of a *socius*
who had been defrauded, or who considered that the
agreement of partnership had been violated, or who
wished for an account or a dissolution, was either an
actio in factum or the more comprehensive *actio pro
socio* [4].

[1] 17 *Dig.* 1. 48.   [2] 17 *Dig.* 2. 1.
[3] 17 *Dig.* 2. 5.   [4] Cic. *Rosc. Com.* 9.

Both these actions were of praetorian origin, and the former was doubtless the experimental mode of relief which prepared the way for the introduction of the latter. At first we may fairly suppose the Praetor to have granted an *actio in factum* adapted to the particular case, with a formula worded somewhat as follows: *Si paret N^m N^m cum A^o A^o pactum conuentum[1] fecisse de societate ad rem certam emendam ideoque renuntiauisse societati ut solus emeret[2], quanti ea res est tantam pecuniam, iudex, N^m N^m A^o A^o condemna. s. n. p. a.* When the *pactum societatis* had thus been protected, and the juristic mind had grown accustomed to regard *societas* in the light of a contract, the Praetor then doubtless announced in his Edict that he would grant an *actio pro socio* to any aggrieved member of a *societas*. In this way agreements of partnership became fully recognised as contracts, and were provided with an *actio in ius concepta*, the formula of which must have been thus expressed[3]:

Quod A^s Agerius cum N^o Negidio societatem coiit universorum quae ex quaestu veniunt, quidquid ob eam rem N^m Negidium A^o Agerio (or *alterum alteri*) *pro socio dare facere praestare oportet ex fide bona, eius iudex N^m Negidium A^o Agerio* (or *alterum alteri*) *condemna. s. n. p. a.*

The superiority of this *bonae fidei* action to the former remedy, as a mode of adjusting complicated disputes arising out of a partnership, is too obvious to require explanation. The *actio in*

[1] 17 *Dig*. 2. 71.   [2] 17 *Dig*. 2. 65. fr. 4.
[3] Lenel, *Ed. Perp.* p. 237.

factum may still however have proved useful in certain cases.

Societas appears in Plautus with much less distinctness than either of the other three consensual contracts. *Socius* is not used by him in a technical or commercial sense, but means only companion[1], or co-owner[2]. The nearest approach to an allusion to *societas* in its more recent form is to be found in *Rudens*[3] where the shares of *socii* are mentioned; but this is no reason for supposing that Plautus knew of *societas* as a contract. The date of the *actio pro socio* is impossible to fix, though Voigt[4] has suggested that the Praetor P. Rutilius Rufus must have been its author in the year 646[5]. Absolute certainty on the subject is unattainable, because we cannot tell whether this Rutilius originated or merely mentioned the edict, nor can we positively identify him with the Praetor of A.V.C. 646. On these points there is hopeless controversy[6], so that they must remain unsettled. But what we can do with a certain measure of accuracy, is to trace the process by which *societas* came to be regarded as a contractual relation, and slowly grew in importance till it called for the creation by the Praetor of a *bonae fidei* action to protect it. This action certainly existed about the end of the seventh century, for it is mentioned in the *Lex Iulia Municipalis* of

[1] *Bacch.* 5. 1. 19 ; *Cist.* 4. 2. 78.
[2] *Rud.* 4. 3. 95.   [3] 1. 4. 20 and 2. 6. 67.
[4] *Ius N.* IV. 603 note 204.
[5] 38 *Dig.* 2. 1.
[6] See Huschke, *Z. für Civ. und Proc.* 14. 19 ; Schilling, *Inst.* § 313.

A.V.C. 709[1], and was discussed by Quintus Mucius
Scaeuola[2]. A closer approximation to the date of
its origin seems to be impossible.

1. *Societas omnium bonorum.*

The original conception of *societas* seems not to
have been that of a commercial combination, but of
a family. Not indeed that the term *societas* was
ever applied to the association of father, mother,
children and cognates; but they were practically
regarded as a single body, each member of which
was bound by solemn ties to share the good or bad
fortune which befell the rest. The duty of avenging
the death of a blood-relation, the duty of providing
a certain portion for children, as enforced by the
querela inofficiosi testamenti, the *obsequia* which
children owed to their parents, are illustrations of
the principle. Now this body, the family, could
hold common property: and here is the point at
which the family touches the institution of partnership. The technical term which expressed the
tenancy in common of brothers in the family property (*hereditas*), was *consortium*[3], and the brother
co-tenants were called *consortes*. This institution
of *consortium* was of great antiquity, being even
found in the *Sutras*[4]. It is compared by Gellius[5]
to the relation of *societas*, and arose from the
descent or devise of the patrimonial estate to several
children who held it undivided. Division might at
any time be made among them by the *actio familiae*

---

[1] Bruns, *Font.* p. 107.   [2] Gai. III. 149; Cic. *Off.* III. 17. 70.
[3] Cic. 2 *Verr.* II. 3. 23; Paul. Diac. 72.
[4] Leist, *Alt.-Ar. Ius Gent.* p. 414.   [5] I. 9. 12.

erciscundae[1], but they might often prefer to continue the *consortium,* either because the property was small, or because they wished to carry on an established family business. If the latter course was adopted, the tenancy in common became a partnership, embracing in its assets the whole wealth of the partners; and it is easy to see how this natural partnership, if found to be advantageous, would soon be copied by voluntary associations of strangers. Thus *socius,* as we know from Cicero[2], was often used as a synonym of *consors,* and there can be no doubt that *consortium* was the original pattern of the *societas omnium bonorum*[3]. That there were some differences between the rules of *consortium* and those of *societas* does not affect the question. For instance[4], the gains of the *consortes* were not brought into the common stock, but those of *socii* were; while the death of a *socius* dissolved the *societas,* but that of a *consors* did not[5] dissolve the *consortium.* These points of difference and others[6] probably arose from the juristic interpretation applied to *societas,* when it had once become fairly recognised as a purely commercial contract. But *consortium* and *societas omnium bonorum* have two points in common which show that they must have been historically connected. (i) In *societas omnium bonorum* there was a complete and immediate transfer of property from the individuals to the *societas*[7], whereas the obligations of

---

[1] Paul. Diac. *s. u. erctum.*   [2] *Brut.* I. 2.
[3] Leist, *Soc.* 24 ; Pernice, *Z. der S. Stift. R. A.* III. 85.
[4] 17 *Dig.* 2. 52.   [5] Pernice, *Labeo* I. p. 69.
[6] See Pernice, *Labeo* I. 85-6.   [7] 17 *Dig.* 2. 1.

each remained distinct and were not shared by the others[1]. Now this is exactly what would have happened in *consortium* : the property would have been common, but the obligation of each *consors* would have remained peculiar to himself. (ii) The treatment of *socii* as brothers[2] is clearly also a reminiscence of *consortium* ; and this conception of *fraternitas*, being peculiar to the *societas omnium bonorum*[3], makes its connection with the old *consortium* still more evident.

The fraternal character of this particular *societas* is responsible for the existence of a generous rule which subsequently, under the Empire, became extended so as to apply to the other kinds of *societas*[4]. The rule was that no defendant in an *actio pro socio* should be condemned to make good any claim beyond the actual extent of his means[5]. This was known as the *beneficium competentiae* ; and it gave rise to a qualified formula for the *actio pro socio*, as follows :

Quod A[s] Agerius cum N[o] Negidio societatem omnium bonorum coiit, quidquid ob eam rem N[m] Negidium A[o] Agerio dare f. p. oportet ex f. b. dumtaxat in id quod N[s] Negidius facere potest, quodue dolo malo fecerit quominus possit, eius iudex N[m] Negidium A[o] Agerio condemna. s. n. p. a.

2.   *Societas negotii uel rei alicuius.*

This second form of partnership must have been the most common, since it was presumed to be intended whenever the term *societas* was alone used[6].

---

[1] 17 *Dig.* 2. 3.   [2] 17 *Dig.* 2. 63.   [3] 17 *Dig.* 2. 63.
[4] 17 *Dig.* 2. 63. fr. 1.   [5] 42 *Dig.* 1. 16 and 22.
[6] 17 *Dig.* 2. 7.

It has also been derived from *consortium* by Lastig[1]. His theory is that *consortes*, or brothers, when they undertook a business in partnership with one another[2], often modified their relations by agreement. The special agreement, he thinks, then became the conspicuous feature of the partnership, and the relations thus established were copied by associations not of *consortes* but of strangers. The object of the theory is to explain the correal obligation of partners. This correality did not however exist at Rome[3], except in the case of banking partnerships, where we are told that it was a peculiar rule made by custom[4], so that Lastig's theory lacks point. A further objection[5] is that this theory does not explain, but is absolutely inconsistent with, the existence of the *actio pro socio* as an *actio famosa*. The fraternal relations existing between *consortes* could never have suggested such a remedy, for Cicero in his defence of Quinctius lays great stress on the enormity of the brother's conduct in having brought such a humiliating action against his client.

Another explanation of the *actio pro socio* is given by Leist[6]. He derives it from the *actio societatis* given by the Praetor against freedmen who refused to share their earnings with their patrons. This *societas* of the patron must have been a one-sided privilege, like his right to the freedman's

---

[1] *Z. für ges. Handelsrecht.* xxiv. 409–428.

[2] As in 26 *Dig.* 7. 47. 6.

[3] 14 *Dig.* 3. 13. 2 ; 17 *Dig.* 2. 82.

[4] Auct. ad Her. ii. 13. 19 ; 2 *Dig.* 14. 9.

[5] As Pernice has pointed out, *Labeo* i. p. 94.

[6] *Soc.* p. 32.

services[1]; for the freedman could never have brought an action against his patron, since he was not entitled to any share in the patron's property. The *actio societatis* was therefore a penal remedy available only to the patron, and consequently it cannot possibly have suggested the bilateral *actio pro socio* of partners. Nor can the *bonae fidei* character of the *actio pro socio* be explained if we assume such an origin.

The most reasonable view appears to be that which regards the *actio pro socio* as the outcome of necessity. The Praetor saw partnerships springing up about him in the busy life of Rome. He saw that the mutual relations of *socii* were unregulated by law, as those of *adpromissores* had been before the legislation described above in Chapter v. He found that an *actio in factum*, based on the Edict *Pacta conuenta*, was but an imperfect remedy; and as an addition to the Edict was then the simplest method of correcting the law, it was most natural for him to institute an *actio pro socio*, in which *bona fides* was made one of the chief requisites simply because the mutual relations of *socii* had hitherto been based upon *fides*[2].

3. *Societas uectigalium uel publicanorum.*

This kind of *societas* was a corporation rather than a partnership, and we have proof in Livy that such corporations existed long before the other kinds of *societas* came to be recognised as contracts. These

[1] 38 *Dig.* 2. 1.

[2] Cic. *Quint.* 6. 26 ; *Q. Rosc.* 6. 16 ; *S. Rosc.* 40. 116 ; 2 *Verr.* III. 58. 134.

societates acted as war-contractors[1], collectors of taxes[2], and undertakers of public works[3]. In one passage in Livy[4] they are called *redemtores*, and we find three *societates* during the second Punic War in A.V.C. 539[5] supplying the State with arms, clothes and corn. It was perhaps the success of these *societates publicanorum*[6] which introduced the conception of commercial and voluntary partnership. But still they were utterly unlike partnerships[7], so that their history must have been quite different from that of the other *societates*. They were probably derived from the ancient *sodalitates* or *collegia*[8], which were perpetual associations, either religious (e.g. *augurium collegia*), or administrative (*quaestorum collegia*), or for mutual benefit, like the guilds of the Middle Ages (*fabrorum collegia*). This theory of their origin is based upon three points of strong resemblance which seem to justify us in establishing a close connection between *societas* and *collegium*:

(1)   Both were regulated by law[9], and were established only by State concessions or charters.

(2)   Both had a perpetual corporate existence, and were not dissolved by the death of any one member[10].

(3)   Both were probably of Greek origin. We

---

[1] Liu. xxxiv. 6 in A.V.C. 559.   [2] Liu. xxvii. 3 (A.V.C. 544).

[3] Liu. xxiv. 18 (A.V.C. 540); Cic. 2 *Verr.* i. 50. 150.

[4] xlii. 3 (A.V.C. 581).   [5] Liu. xxiii. 48–9.

[6] Liu. xxxix. 44; xxv. 3.   [7] 3 *Dig.* 4. 1.

[8] *Lex rep.* of A.V.C. 631, cap. 10; Cic. *leg. agr.* ii. 8. 21; *pro domo* 20. 51; *Planc.* 15. 36.

[9] Gaius, 3 *Dig.* 4. 1; 47 *Dig.* 22. 1.

[10] 28 *Dig.* 5. 59 fr. 1; 17 *Dig.* 2. 59; Cic. *Brut.* i. 1.

are told that *societates publicanorum* existed at Athens[1], while Gaius[2] derives from a law of Solon the rule applying to all *collegia*, that they might make whatever bye-laws they pleased, provided these did not conflict with the public law.

These three facts may well lead us to derive this particular form of *societas* from the *collegium*. We know further that the jurists looked upon it as quite different from the ordinary *societas*, and that it did not have the *actio pro socio* as a remedy[3]. The president or head of the *societas* was called *manceps*[4], or *magister* if he dealt with third parties[5], and the modes of suretyship which it used in its corporate transactions were *praedes* and *praedia*[6], another mark perhaps of its semi-public origin.

[1] Arist. *Rep. Ath.* 52. 3 and cf. Voigt, *I. N.* II. 401.

[2] 47 *Dig.* 22. 4.   [3] Voigt, *Röm. RG.* I. 808.

[4] Ps. Asc. in Cic. *Diu.*; Paul. Diac. 151 *s. u. manceps*; Cic. *dom.* 10. 25; Cic. *Planc.* 26. 64.

[5] Paul. Diac. *s. u. magisterare*; Cic. *Att.* v. 5. 3; Cic. 2 *Verr.* II. 70. 169; *ib.* III. 71. 167.

[6] *Lex Mal.* c. 65.

CHAPTER VII.

Real Contracts.

Art. 1. MVTVVM. We have not yet really disposed of all the consensual contracts, for we now come to a class of obligations entered into without formality and by the mere consent of the parties, but in which that consent was signified in one particular way, i.e. by the delivery of the object in respect of which the contract was made. The contracts of this class have therefore been termed Real contracts, though they might with equal propriety be called Consensual. The oldest of them all is *mutuum*, the gratuitous loan of *res fungibiles*, and it stands apart from the other contracts of its class in such a marked way, that its peculiarities can only be understood from its history. It differed from the other so-called real contracts, (i) in having for its remedy the *condictio*, an *actio stricti iuris*; (ii) in being the only one which conveyed ownership in the objects lent, and did not require them to be returned *in specie*. Both peculiarities require explanation.

12—2

The most important function of Contract in early times was the making of money loans, and for this the Romans had three devices peculiarly their own, first *nexum*, then *sponsio*, and lastly *expensilatio*. But these were available only to Roman citizens, so that the legal reforms constituting the so-called *ius gentium* naturally included new methods of performing this particular transaction. One such innovation was the modification of *sponsio*, already described, and the rise of *stipulatio* in its various forms : another was the recognition of an agreement followed by a payment as constituting a valid contract, which might be enforced by the *condictio*, like the older *sponsio* and *expensilatio*. This latter innovation was the contract known as *mutuum*. It doubtless originated in custom, and was crystallised in the Edict of some reforming Praetor.

As its object was money, or things analogous to money in having no individual importance, such as corn, seeds, &c., the object naturally did not have to be returned *in specie* by the borrower.

Though the bare agreement to repay was sufficiently binding as regards the principal sum, the payment of interest on the loan could not be provided for by bare agreement, but had to be clothed in a stipulation. This rule may have been due to the fact that *mutuum* was originally a loan from friend to friend; but it rather seems to indicate that bare *consensus* was at first somewhat reluctantly tolerated.

In Plautus *mutuum* appears as a gratuitous loan, generally made between friends [1] and in sharp con-

---

[1] *Curc.* 1. 1. 67 and 2. 3. 51 ; *Pseud.* 1. 3. 76.

trast to *foenus*, a loan with interest[1], which was always entered into by stipulation. When *mutuum* is used by Plautus to denote a loan on which interest is payable, we must therefore understand that a special agreement to that effect had been entered into by stipulation, since *mutuum* was essentially gratuitous.

From three passages[2] it is evident that *mutuum* was recoverable by action in the time of Plautus[3] (circ. A. V. C. 570), and it seems probable that Livy[4] also uses it in a technical sense[5]. If then we place the date of the *Lex Aebutia* as late as A.V.C. 513, and suppose, as Voigt does[6], that *mutuum* being a *iuris gentium* contract must have been subsequent to that law, we shall be led to conclude that *mutuum* came into use about the second quarter of the sixth century. This theory as to date is supported by the fact, which Karsten points out[7], that *mutuum* would hardly have been possible without a uniform legal tender, and that Rome did not appropriate to herself the exclusive right of coinage till A.V.C. 486. We thus see that the introduction of *mutuum* and that of *emtio uenditio*, i.e. of the first real and the first consensual contract, took place at about the same time.

As regards its peculiar remedy we know that money lent by *mutuum* was recoverable by a *condictio certae pecuniae*, with the usual *sponsio* and

---

[1] *Asin.* 1. 3. 95.
[2] *Trin.* 3. 2. 101; 4. 3. 44; *Bacch.* 2. 3. 16.
[3] *Curc.* A.V.C. 560.   [4] XXXII. 2. 1.   [5] Of A.V.C. 555.
[6] *I. N.* IV. 614.   [7] *Stip.* p. 38.

restipulatio tertiae partis[1]. It seems, like *expensilatio*, to have received this stringent remedy by means of juristic interpretation, which extended the meaning and the remedy of *pecunia certa credita* so as to cover this new form of loan. Thus we find *credere* often used by Plautus in the sense of making a *mutuum*[2].

When this final extension had been made in the meaning of *pecunia credita*, we may reconstruct the Edict on that subject as follows[3]:

SI CERTVM PETETVR DE PECVNIA QVAM QVIS CREDIDERIT EXPENSVMVE TVLERIT MVTVOVE DEDERIT NEVE EX IVSTA CAVSA SOLVERIT PROMISERITVE, DE EO IVDICIVM DABO. The *iudicium* here referred to was the *condictio certae pecuniae*, the formula of which has already been given[4].

We know that *mutuum* could be applied to other fungible things besides money, such as wine, oil or seeds, and in those cases the remedy must have been the *condictio triticaria*[5].

FOENVS NAVTICVM (δάνειον ναυτικόν). A contract very similar to *mutuum*, which we know to have existed in the Republican period, since we find it mentioned by Seruius Sulpicius[6] and entered into by Cato[7], was *foenus nauticum*, a form of marine insurance resembling bottomry[8]. It consisted of a money loan (*pecunia traiecticia*) to be paid back by the borrower,—invariably the owner of a ship,—

---

[1] Cic. *Rosc. Com.* 4. 13.

[2] As in *Pers.* 1. 1. 37; *Merc.* 1. 1. 58; *Pseud.* 1. 5. 91.

[3] Voigt, *I. N.* iv. 616.   [4] p. 104.   [5] 12 *Dig.* 1. 2.

[6] 22 *Dig.* 2. 8.   [7] Plutarch, *Cat. Mai.* 21.

[8] Carnazza, *Dir. Com.* p. 176 ff.

only in the event of the ship's safe return from her voyage. A slave or freedman of the lender apparently went with the ship to guard against fraud[1]; but there was no hypothecation of the ship, as in a modern bottomry bond.

The contract resembled *mutuum* in being made without formality; but its marked peculiarities were:

(i) That it was confined to loans of money,

(ii) And to loans from insurers to ship-owners,

(iii) And because of the great risk it was not a gratuitous loan, but always bore interest at a very high rate[2]. It is, however, quite possible that this interest was not originally allowed as a part of the formless contract, but that it was customary, as Labeo states[3], to stipulate for a severe *poena* in case the loan was not returned. If that be so, the stipulatory *poena* spoken of by Seruius and Labeo must have been the forerunner in the Republican period of the onerous interest mentioned by Paulus[4] as an inherent part of this contract in his day.

Art. 2. COMMODATVM. The next three real contracts are not mentioned by Gaius, who apparently took his classification from Seruius Sulpicius, and it therefore seems certain that in the time of Seruius and during the Republic they were not regarded as contracts, but as mere *pacta praetoria*.

Commodatum was the same transaction as *mutuum* applied to a different object. In *mutuum* there was a gratuitous loan of money or other *res fungibilis*,

---

[1] Plut. *Cat.* l. c.; 45 *Dig.* 1. 122 fr. 1.

[2] 22 *Dig.* 2. 7.   [3] 22 *Dig.* 2. 9.   [4] 22 *Dig.* 2. 7.

whereas in *commodatum* the gratuitous loan was one
of a *res non fungibilis* [1].

Both were originally acts of friendship, as their
gratuitous nature implies. Plautus shows us that in
his day the loan of money was not distinguished from
that of other objects, for he uses *commodare* [2] and
utendum dare [3] in speaking of a money loan, as well
as in describing genuine cases of *commodatum*. We
do not, however, discover from Plautus that *commodatum* was actionable in his time, as *mutuum* clearly
was. *Vtendum dare*, we may note, is in his plays
a more usual term than *commodare* [4]. If it be asked
why the *condictio* was not extended to *commodatum*
as it was to *mutuum*, the answer is that the latter
always gave rise to a liquidated debt, whereas in a
case of *commodatum* the damages had first to be
judicially ascertained, and for this purpose the *condictio* was manifestly not available.

The earliest mention of *commodatum* as an actionable agreement occurs in the writings of Quintus
Mucius Scaeuola (ob. A.V.C. 672) quoted by Ulpian [5]
and Gellius [6]. Cicero significantly omits to mention
it in his list of *bonae fidei* contracts, and the *Lex Iulia
Municipalis* (A.V.C. 709) contains no allusion to it [7].
The peculiar rules of the agreement seem to have
become fixed at an early date. Quintus Mucius
Scaeuola is said to have decided that *culpa leuis*

---

[1] e.g. a *scyphus*, Plaut. *Asin.* 2. 4. 38 or a *chlamys*, *Men.* 4. 4.
94.

[2] *Asin.* 3. 3. 135.   [3] *Persa*, 1. 3. 37.
[4] *Aul.* 1. 2. 18; *Rud.* 3. 1. 9.   [5] 13 *Dig.* 6. 5.
[6] vi. 15. 2.   [7] Bruns, *Font.* p. 107.

should be the measure of responsibility required from the bailee (*is cui commodatur*), and to have established the rule as to *furtum usus,* in cases where the *res commodata* was improperly used. It seems therefore probable that the Praetor recognised *commodatum* at first as a *pactum praetorium,* and granted for its protection an *actio in factum* with the following formula :

Si paret A^m Agerium N^o Negidio rem qua de agitur commodasse (or *utendam dedisse*) *eamque A^o Agerio redditam non esse, quanti ea res erit, tantam pecuniam N^m Negidium A^o Agerio condemna. s. n. p. a.*

The agreement between bailor and bailee probably did not come to be regarded as a regular contract until after the time of Cicero. We must therefore place the introduction of the *actio commodati* at least as late as A.V.C. 710, and by so doing we explain Cicero's silence. Whatever conclusion we shall arrive at as to *depositum* must almost necessarily be taken as applying to *commodatum* also. They both had double forms of action in the time of Gaius[1], neither is mentioned by Cicero, and Scaeuola evidently dealt with them both together. Hence their simultaneous origin seems almost certain. The *actio commodati* is said to have been instituted by a Praetor Pacuuius[2], who, like Plautus, used the words *utendum dare* instead of *commodare.* The terms of his Edict must therefore have been :

---

[1] IV. 47.   [2] 13 *Dig.* 6. 1.

QVOD QVIS VTENDVM DEDISSE DICETVR, DE EO
IVDICIVM DABO [1].

The author of this Edict was formerly supposed
by Voigt to be Pacuuius Antistius Labeo [2], the
father of Labeo the jurist; but this statement has
recently been withdrawn [3] on the ground that this
Pacuuius, having been a pupil of Seruius Sulpicius [4],
could not have been Praetor as early as the time of
Quintus Mucius. If however the above theory as to
the dates be correct, Voigt's former view may be
sound : Q. Mucius may have been speaking of the
actionable *pactum*, while Pacuuius may have been
the author of the true contract. The *actio commodati directa* had a formula as follows : *Quod A[s]
Agerius N[o] Negidio rem q. d. a. commodauit* (or
utendam dedit) *quidquid ob eam rem N[m] Negidium A[o] Agerio dare facere praestare oportet ex
fide bona, eius iudex N[m] Negidium A[o] Agerio condemna. s. n. p. a.* It was doubtless in this form
that the action on a *commodatum* was unknown to
Cicero. He must have been familiar only with the
actio in factum, and for that very reason he must
have regarded *commodatum* not as a contract, but as
a *pactum conuentum*.

Art. 3. DEPOSITVM. The most general word
denoting the bestowal of a trust by one person
upon another was *commendare* [5], and Voigt has
shown [6] that *commendatum* was the technical term

---

[1] *I. N.* iii. 969. [2] *I. N.* iii. 969 note 1496.
[3] *R. RG.* i. 622 note 25. [4] 1 *Dig.* 2. 2. 44.
[5] Plaut. *Trin.* 4. 3. 76 ; Cic. *Fam.* ii. 6. 5 ; 16 *Dig.* 3. 24 ; Cic.
Fin. iii. 2. 9. [6] *R. RG.* i. App. 5.

for a particular kind of *pactum*. If the object of *commendatio*[1] was the performance of some service, the relation was a case of *mandatum*[2]: if its object was the keeping of some article in safe custody, the relation was described as *depositum*[3]. This case clearly shows how arbitrary is the distinction drawn by the Roman jurists between Real and Consensual Contract. Though starting, as we have seen, from the same point, *mandatum* came to be classed as a consensual, and *depositum* as a real contract. This was simply because the latter dealt, while the former did not deal, with the possession of a definite *res*.

Depositum distinctly appears in Plautus[4] as an agreement by which some object is placed in a man's custody and committed to his care, though *deponere* is not the word generally used by Plautus to denote the act of depositing. He prefers the phrase *seruandum dare*, corresponding to *utendum dare*, which we found to be his usual expression for *commodatum*[5]. These very words, *seruandum dare*, were also used by Quintus Mucius Scaeuola in discussing *depositum*[6], but we cannot ascertain from his language whether or not the *actio depositi* was already known to him. He may merely have been discussing an actionable *pactum*. Nor can we infer from any passage of Plautus the existence of *depositum* as a contract in his time. He seems

---

[1] Cic. *Fin.* III. 20. 65.   [2] Plaut. *Merc.* 5. 1. 6.
[3] 16 *Dig.* 3. 24; Plaut. *Merc.* 2. 1. 22.   [4] *Bacch.* 2. 3. 72.
[5] *Merc.* 2. 1. 14; *Curc.* 2. 3. 66; *Bacch.* 2. 3. 10.
[6] Gell. VI. 15. 2.

rather to represent it, as Cicero does[1], in the light of a friendly relation based simply on *fides*[2]; and in most of the Plautine passages the transaction is that which was afterwards known as *depositum irregulare,* i.e. the deposit of a package containing money either at a banker's[3], or with a friend[4].

Some have thought that there must have been an action in Plautus' time for the protection of such important trusts[5], but Demelius[6] points out that the *actio furti* (to which Paulus alludes as *actio ex causa depositi*) would have afforded ample protection in most cases; and it would be extremely rash to infer that either *commodatum* or *depositum* was actionable in the sixth century of the City.

At first sight it even looks as though *depositum* was not protected by any action in the days of Cicero. The passages in which he mentions it[7] appear to treat the restoration of the *res deposita* rather as a moral than a legal duty. Similarly where he enumerates the *bonae fidei* actions[8], where he mentions the persons *qui bonam fidem praestare debent*[9], and where he describes the *iudicia de fide mala*[10], he entirely leaves out the *actio depositi* and does not make the slightest allusion to *depositum.*

But all this is equally true of *commodatum*[11]. And since we have the clearest evidence that *commodatum* was actionable in the time of Quintus

[1] 2 *Verr.* IV. 16. 36.   [2] *Merc.* 2. 1. 14.
[3] *Curc.* 2. 3. 66.   [4] *Bacch.* 2. 3. 101.
[5] Costa, *Dir. Priv.* p. 320.   [6] *Z. für RG.* II. 224.
[7] *Parad.* III. 1. 21; *Off.* I. 10. 31; III. 25. 95.
[8] *Off.* III. 17. 70.   [9] *Top.* 10. 42.
[10] *N. D.* III. 30. 7.   [11] Gai. IV. 47.

Mucius Scaeuola[1], we can hardly avoid the conviction that *depositum* also was actionable in his day by means of an *actio in factum*, whereas the *actio depositi* was not introduced, as Voigt holds, till the beginning of the eighth century[2].

This theory of development, already applied to *mandatum* and *societas*, has the advantage, not only of explaining why *commodatum* and *depositum* were not numbered among *bonae fidei contractus*, but also of accounting for the existence in Gaius' day of their double formulae which have puzzled so many jurists[3]. We may then believe that *depositum* was first made actionable between A.V.C. 650 and 670 as a *pactum praetorium*, and with the protection of an *actio in factum concepta* as given by Gaius: *Si paret A^m Agerium apud N^m Negidium mensam argenteam deposuisse eamque dolo N^i Negidii A^o Agerio redditam non esse, quanti ea res erit, tantam pecuniam, iudex, N^m Negidium A^o Agerio condemnato. s. n. p. a.*

This formula was doubtless the only one provided for *depositum* down to the end of Cicero's career. But about A.V.C. 710[4] juristic interpretation began to regard *commodatum* and *depositum* as genuine contracts *iuris ciuilis*, and thereupon a second formula was introduced into the Edict, without disturbing the earlier one, so that *depositum*, like *commodatum*, was finally recognised as a contract.

[1] 13 *Dig.* 6. 5. [2] *Röm. RG.* I. 623.

[3] See Muirhead's *Gaius*, p. 293 note.

[4] 41 *Dig.* 2. 3. 18 ; 16 *Dig.* 31. 1. 46 ; Trebatius was *trib. pleb.* A.V.C. 707.

We know that the Praetor's Edict by which this change was brought about ran somewhat thus: QVOD NEQVE TVMVLTVS NEQVE INCENDII NEQVE RVINAE NEQVE NAVFRAGII CAVSA DEPOSITVM SIT IN SIMPLVM, EARVM AVTEM RERVM QVAE SVPRA COMPREHENSAE SVNT IN IPSVM IN DVPLVM, IN HEREDEM EIVS QVOD DOLO MALO FACTVM ESSE DICETVR QVI MORTVVS SIT IN SIMPLVM, QVOD IPSIVS IN DVPLVM IVDICIVM DABO[1]. The penalty of *duplum* shows that, where the *depositum* had been compelled by adverse circumstances, a violation of the contract was regarded as peculiarly disgraceful and treacherous. In other cases, where the *depositum* was made under ordinary circumstances, the amount recovered was *simplum*, and the new formula must have been that given by Gaius[2] as follows: *Quod A[s] Agerius apud N[m] Negidium mensam argenteam deposuit qua de re agitur, quidquid ob eam rem N[m] Negidium A[o] Agerio dare facere oportet ex fide bona, eius iudex N[m] Negidium A[o] Agerio condemnato. s. n. p. a.*

Art. 4. PIGNVS. The giving and taking of a pledge appears in Plautus as a means of securing a promise, but seems then to have belonged to the class of friendly acts which the law did not condescend to enforce. In *Captiui*[3] for instance, the slave who had been pledged is demanded in a purely informal way, and in *Rudens*[4] *pignus* is a mere token given to prove that the giver is speaking the truth. Its connection with *arrhabo* is very close. Each served to show that an agreement was seriously

[1] 16 *Dig.* 3. 1.	[2] IV. 47.
[3] 5. 1. 18.	[4] 2. 7. 23.

meant by the parties, or was a means of securing
credit as a substitute for money[1], and if the agreement was broken, the *pignus* or *arrhabo* was doubtless
kept as compensation. This practice of giving pawns
or pledges was probably of great antiquity, but we
hear nothing of it from legal sources, simply because
it was an institution founded on *mores* alone. It probably applied only to moveables and *res nec mancipi*[2],
for *res mancipi* could be dealt with by a *pactum
fiduciae* annexed to *mancipatio*. Gaius[3] derives the
word from *pugnum*, because a pledge was *handed*
over to the pledgee; but the correct derivation is
doubtless from the same root as *pactum, pepigi,
Pacht, Pfand*[4]. *Pignus* must then have meant a
thing fixed or fastened, and so a security. And
this derivation suits the word in the phrase *pignoris
capio* equally well, without leading us to suppose that
the custom of giving a pledge was in any way derived
from the *pignoris capio* of the *legis actio* system.

We do not know when *pignus* became a contract,
though it certainly was so before the end of the
Republic. Long before being recognised as such it
doubtless enjoyed the protection of an *actio in factum*,
with a formula as follows: *Si paret A^m Agerium N^o
Negidio ratem q. d. a. ob pecuniam debitam pignori
dedisse, eamque pecuniam solutam, eoue nomine satisfactum esse, aut per N^m Negidium stetisse quominus
soluatur, eamque ratem q. d. a. A^o Agerio redditam
non esse, quanti ea res erit, tantam, &c.*[5] In course

---

[1] Bechmann, *Kauf*, ii. 416.   [2] 50 *Dig.* 16. 238.   [3] *ibid.*

[4] Dernburg, *Pfr.* i. p. 49; *Beitr. zur vrgl. Sprachforsch.* ii. p. 49.

[5] Lenel, *Ed. perp.* p. 201.

of time the *actio pigneraticia* was introduced as an
alternative remedy, and Ubbelohde [1] has argued that
since its place in the edict was between *commodatum*
and *depositum*, the Praetor must have introduced
the *actio pigneraticia* after the *actio commodati* and
before the *actio depositi*; which seems a very plausible conjecture. We have no direct evidence of the
existence of an *actio pigneraticia* earlier than the
time of Alfenus Varus, a jurist of the later Republic [2]; it is not mentioned by Cicero; in short
everything points to the origin of the contract of
pignus as corresponding in age to that of *commodatum* and *depositum*. The language of the Edict
by which *pignus* was made a contract has not
survived, while the formula of its *actio pigneraticia*
resembled of course that of the *actio depositi*, and
need not therefore be given.

Though *pignus* was doubtless a very inadequate
security from the point of view of the pledgor, since
it might at any time be alienated or destroyed, it is
the only form which appears to be common in
Plautus, and of *fiducia* he shows us not a trace [3].
Pignus seems to have been much used for making
wagers, and *pignore certare* was probably as common
as *sponsione certare* [4], which we treated of in a previous article.

The contracts of a kindred nature which seem to
have arisen even sooner than *pignus* will be discussed
in the next chapter.

[1] *G. der ben. Realcont.* p. 62. [2] 13 *Dig.* 7. 30.
[3] Costa, *Dir. Priv.* p. 262. [4] Bekker, *Akt.* I. 253.

CHAPTER VIII.

CONTRACTS NOT USUALLY CLASSIFIED AS SUCH.

Art. 1. FIDVCIA. We have examined in a former chapter the early origin of the *pactum fiduciae*[1], a formless agreement annexed to a solemn conveyance, by which the transferee of the object conveyed as security agreed to reconvey, as soon as the debt was paid, or whenever a given condition should arise. As a result of the Edict *Pacta conuenta*, and before Cicero's time[2], this *pactum* became enforceable by the *actio fiduciae*.

This action was *in factum*, like the others of its class, and its function was to award damages, but it could not otherwise compel the actual reconveyance of the object. Its formula must have been worded as follows[3]:

Si paret A^m Agerium N^o Negidio fundum quo de agitur ob pecuniam debitam fiduciae causa mancipio dedisse, eamque pecuniam solutam eoue nomine satisfactum esse, aut per N^m Negidium stetisse quominus solueretur, eumque fundum redditum non esse, nego-

---

[1] *Supra*, p. 78.   [2] Cic. *Off.* III. 15. 61.
[3] Lenel, *Ed. Perp.* p. 233.

tiumue ita actum non esse ut inter bonos bene agier
oportet et sine fraudatione, quanti ea res erit tantam
pecuniam iudex N^m Negidium A° Agerio condemna.
s. n. p. a.

The peculiar clause "*ut inter bonos bene agier*
oportet"[1] virtually made this a *bonae fidei* action.
That fact may perhaps explain why *fiducia* was never
protected by a formula *in ius concepta*, and hence
was never regarded as a true contract.

Art. 2. HYPOTHECA. We have seen that there
were two ways in which a tangible security might be
given: (i) the object might be conveyed with a
pactum fiduciae, providing that it should be recon-
veyed on the fulfilment of a certain condition, or
else (ii) the mere detention of the object might be
granted on similar terms. In the former case
the pledge or its value could be recovered by
the *actio fiduciae*, in the latter by the *actio pigne-*
raticia whose origin we have just discussed. But
neither *fiducia* nor *pignus* was a contract of pledge
pure and simple; each consisted of an agreement
plus a delivery of the object.

The abstract conception of mortgage, i.e. pledging
by mere agreement, is a distinct advance upon both
these methods. The contract which embodied this
form of pledge was known as *hypotheca*; and as its
name indicates it was borrowed from the Greeks,
from whom the Romans also took the *Lex Rhodia*
de iactu and the *foenus nauticum*. Precisely the
same contract is found in the speeches of Demos-

---

[1] Cic. *Top.* 17. 66.

thenes[1] under the name of ὑποθήκη, which could be applied to moveables or immoveables, and even to articles not yet in existence. The Romans however regarded *hypotheca* not as a contract but as a *pactum*.

It is quite certain that a legal conception so refined as the *pactum hypothecae* could not have had a place in the legal system of the XII Tables. There are passages in Festus[2] and Dionysius[3] in which the words *si quid pignoris* and ἐνεχυράζειν have been supposed to indicate the existence of some such practice at an early period. But the evidence is much too vague to supply trustworthy data, and we may confidently assert that mortgage was unknown to the early law[4]. Accordingly, we find that *hypotheca* was introduced and made actionable by slow degrees. Its popular name was *pignus oppositum*, as distinct from *pignus depositum*, the ordinary *pignus* above described.

Its introduction seems to have been one of the many legal innovations produced by the large immigration of strangers into Rome after the Second Punic War. These strangers must generally have become tenants of Roman landlords, since the lack of *ius commercii* prevented their buying lands or houses, and in order to secure his rent, the only resource open to the landlord was to take the household goods of these tenants as security. Such household goods (*inuecta illata*) probably constituted in most cases the only wealth of the foreign immigrant, conse-

[1] Dernburg, *Pfdr.* I. p. 69. [2] s.u. *nancitor*.
[3] vi. 29. [4] Dernburg, *Pfdr.* I. 55.

quently the landlord could not remove them, and the method of *pignus* was not available. The expedient which suggested itself was that the tenant should pledge his goods without removal, by means of a simple agreement. The relation thus created was the original form of *hypotheca* and was precisely analogous to that of a modern chattel mortgage.

As the idea was introduced by foreigners[1], it was very natural that this agreement of pledge should have received a foreign name. Another class to whom the new expedient was applied were the free agricultural tenants (*coloni*) whose sole wealth often consisted of their tools and other agricultural stock[2]. The necessity of making a pledge without removal is obvious in their case also.

I.   It was for the protection of landlords that a Praetor Saluius introduced the *interdictum Saluianum*, which seems to have been the first legal recognition that *hypotheca* received. Its date is not known.   Formerly the Praetor Saluius Iulianus, author of the *Edictum perpetuum*, was regarded as the inventor of this interdict, but his own language in the Digest[3] contradicts this supposition.   The most reasonable theory is that the interdict originated before the Edict *Pacta conuenta* (A.V.C. 627) at about the end of the sixth century.

The fact that Plautus knew *hypotheca* as a mere *nudum pactum* can hardly be doubted[4]. It is true that he not only uses, as Terence does a little later[5],

---

[1] Dernburg, *Pfdr.* I. 56.   [2] 4 *Dig.* 15. 3. 1.
[3] 13 *Dig.* 7. 22.   [4] Demelius, *Z. für RG.* II. 232.
[5] *Phorm.* 4. 3. 56.

the phrase *pignori opponere*[1] to denote the making
of a pledge by mere agreement; but he also mentions the Greek technical term ἐπιθήκη and seems
to use *hypotheca* as a metaphor[2]. The testimony
to be gathered from these passages does not however
prove that *hypotheca* was actionable[3].

The contents of the *interdictum Saluianum* cannot be given with certainty. We only know two
things about it: (1) that it was a remedy of limited
scope, being available only against the tenant or
pledgor, but not against third parties to whom he
had transferred or sold or pledged the goods, and
(2) that the interdict was prohibitory and forbade
the pledgor to prevent the landlord from seizing
the objects which had been mortgaged.

(1) This first proposition is distinctly stated by
a constitution of Gordian[4], but flatly contradicted
by a passage in the Digest[5]. The latter authority,
however, seems open to strong suspicion[6] and the
fact that the *actio Seruiana* was presumably introduced because the *interdictum Saluianum* was
inadequate further goes to prove the correctness of
Gordian's constitution.

(2) We may be fairly certain that the interdict
was prohibitory, like the *interdictum utrubi,* and
not restitutory, as Huschke would have it[7]; since
the weight of authority is in favour of the former

[1] *Pseud.* 1. 1. 85.   [2] *Truc.* 2. 1. 4.
[3] Costa, *Dir. priv.* p. 264; Dernburg, *Pfdr.* I. p. 65.
[4] 8 *Cod.* 9. 1.   [5] 43 *Dig.* 33. 1.
[6] Lenel, *Z. der Sav. Stiftung*, R. A. III. 181.
[7] *Studien*, p. 398.

view [1]. We may therefore accept Rudorff's restoration of its formula, which runs as follows [2]: *Si is homo quo de agitur est ex his rebus de quibus inter te et conductorem (colonum, &c. &c.) conuenit, ut quae in eum fundum quo de agitur inducta illata ibi nata factaue essent ea pignori tibi pro mercede eius fundi essent, neque ea merces tibi soluta eoue nomine satisfactum est aut per te stat quominus soluatur, ita quominus eum ducas uim fieri ueto.*

II. The second remedy introduced to enforce the formless agreement of mortgage was the *actio Seruiana*, which was far more efficacious. Its author cannot have been Seruius Sulpicius Rufus, the friend of Cicero, because he never was *Praetor Vrbanus*, and the action must have existed long before his time. The Praetor who devised it was doubtless one of the many Seruii Sulpicii whose names constantly appear in the *fasti consulares*, and its age is probably not much less than that of the *interdictum Saluianum*. The action was certainly younger than the interdict, and an improvement upon it, because the jurists treated the law of mortgage under the head of interdict [3], which indicates that this was the form of the original remedy. We may be sure that the interdict is older than the Edict *Pacta conuenta*, for otherwise it would not have been needed. And as soon as *pacta* were thus legally recognised, it is safe to say that a more perfect remedy for *hypotheca* was sure

[1] Dernburg, *Pfdr.* p. 59; Bachofen, *Pfdr.* p. 13; Keller, *Recension.* p. 977 and Rudorff, *Pfandkl.* p. 210; Lenel, *Ed. Perp.* p. 394.

[2] *Pfandkl.* p. 209. Cf. Rudorff, *Ed. Perp.* 232.

[3] Dernburg, *Pfdr.* I. p. 61.

to be devised. The probability is then that the *actio Seruiana* was one of the first products of the Edict *Pacta conuenta,* partly because we know that the interdict was an imperfect remedy, partly because *hypotheca* was much in vogue at that early date. Thus we may gather from Plautus' allusions that *hypotheca* was already in a well developed state about A.V.C. 570. Cato the Censor[1] also seems to have alluded to it, and Caec. Statius (*ob.* A.V.C. 586), as cited by Festus[2], unquestionably did so. The curious circumstance that Cicero should have mentioned it only twice[3] may perhaps be accounted for by the fact that *pignus* in its looser sense was always a synonym for *hypotheca*[4], and as he mentions it so seldom in its Greek form, we may suppose that the term *hypotheca* was then only just coming into general use. We know that *pignus* in the narrower sense was distinguished by Ulpian from *hypotheca* as sharply as we distinguish a pawn from a mortgage[5], but the earlier writers lead us to infer that the term *pignus oppositum,* or simply *pignus,* was originally the equivalent of *hypotheca.*

The effect of the *actio Seruiana* was probably a mere enlargement of the scope of the *interdictum Saluianum,* giving the landlord a legal hold upon the *inuecta illata* of his tenant even in the possession of third parties. But since the right of thus pledging by agreement was as yet recognised only as between the *colonus* or the house-tenant and his landlord,

[1] *R. R.* 146.
[2] s.u. *reluere.*
[3] *Att.* II. 17 and *Fam.* XIII. 56.
[4] 20 *Dig.* 1. 5.
[5] 13 *Dig.* 7. 9.

hypotheca was a transaction still confined to a small class.

III.   A final improvement was effected, perhaps shortly after the one just mentioned, when the Praetor granted an action on the analogy of the *actio Seruiana*, upon all agreements of pledge of whatever description.   From the creation of this action, known as *actio quasi Seruiana*[1], or *hypothecaria*[2], or simply *Seruiana*[3], dated the introduction of a law of mortgage applicable to objects of all kinds.   The name *hypothecaria*, which we find applied only to the last of these three remedies, implies either that this was the only action available for all forms of *hypotheca*, or else that the Greek term was not introduced until the contract had thus become general.

The formula of the *actio quasi Seruiana* or *hypothecaria* was of course *in factum concepta*[4], because the *pactum hypothecae* never was treated as a *contractus iuris ciuilis,* though it became in reality as binding as any contract.   The words are restored by Lenel[5] as follows, in an action by the mortgagee against a third party: *Si paret inter A^{m} Agerium et Lucium Titium conuenisse ut ea res qua de agitur A^{o} Agerio pignori hypothecaeue esset propter pecuniam debitam, eamque rem tunc cum conueniebat in bonis L^{i} Titii fuisse, eamque pecuniam neque solutam neque eo nomine satisfactum esse neque per A^{m} Agerium stare quominus soluatur, nisi ea res A^{o} Agerio arbitratu tuo*

[1] 4 *Inst.* 6. 7.   [2] 16 *Dig.* 1. 13.
[3] Bachofen, *Pfdr.* p. 28.
[4] *Ed. perp.* p. 397; cf. Dernburg, *Pfdr.* i. p. 78.
[5] *ib.* p. 81 ; cf. Rudorff, *Ed. perp.* 234.

*restituetur, quanti ea res erit, tantam pecuniam iudex
N^m Negidium A° Agerio condemna. s. n. p. a.*

No mortgage can be of much practical use unless
it empowers the creditor to sell the thing pledged,
so as to cover his loss. But it is evident that the
mere pledgee or mortgagee could have had no inherent right to sell or convey what did not belong to
him. This was an advantage possessed by *fiducia,*
since the property was fully conveyed and could
therefore be disposed of as soon as the condition was
broken. The only way out of the difficulty both in
pignus and *hypotheca* was to make a condition of
sale part of the original agreement. This was unnecessary under the Empire [1] when the power of sale
came to be implied in every *hypotheca,* but during
the Republic the power had to be explicitly reserved, or else the vendor was liable for conversion
(*furtum*)[2]. Even Gaius [3] speaks as though a *pactum
de uendendo* was usual in his time. Labeo describes
a sale *ex pacto conuento*[4], but the usual name for the
clause of the agreement containing the power of sale
was *lex commissoria.* When it became possible to
insert such a clause is uncertain, but Dernburg
seems right in maintaining that, as the *lex commissoria* was known to Labeo and to the far more
ancient Greek law, it must certainly have been
customary at Rome long before the end of the
Republic.

[1] 13 *Dig.* 7. 4.
[2] 47 *Dig.* 2. 74; Dernburg, *Pfdr.* I. p. 91.   [3] II. 64.
[4] 20 *Dig.* 1. 35.
[5] *Pfdr.* I. p. 86 as against Bachofen, *Pfdr.* p. 157.

The custom of committing *hypothecae* to writing (*tabulae*), which is indicated by Gaius[1], doubtless prevailed also in the Republican period, the object of the writing being simply to facilitate proof.

When we translate *hypotheca* by the English word mortgage, we must not forget that the latter denotes technically a conveyance defeasible by condition subsequent, closely resembling *fiducia*, whereas the former denoted the mere creation of a lien.

On the other hand it is true that our modern mortgage has lost its original resemblance to *fiducia*, and has now become almost identical with *hypotheca*.

Art. 3. PRAEDIATVRA. This was a peculiar form of suretyship which the Roman jurists never treated as a contract, though it doubtless had a very ancient origin. It was connected with the public *emtiones* and *locationes*, and was the regular method by which contractors or undertakers of public work gave bond to do their work properly.

The transaction resembled the giving of *sponsores* in private law. The friends of the contractor who were willing to be his sureties (*praedes*) appeared before the Praetor or other magistrate, and entered into a verbal contract by which they bound themselves with all that they possessed. The magistrate, we are told, asked each surety " *Praesne es ?* " and the surety answered " *Praes* "[2]. This has every appearance of having been a formal contract like *sponsio*, and it is difficult to accept the view of Mommsen[3], who considers that the publicity of the

---

[1] 20 *Dig.* 1. 4 ; 22 *Dig.* 4. 4.
[2] Paul. Diac. s.u. *Praes.*   [3] *Stadtr. von Salpensa*, p. 468.

transaction leads us to infer its formless character. If we follow him in assuming that *praedes* and *praedia* were purely public institutions, how can we explain the existence of the *praedes litis et uindiciarum,* who certainly appeared in private suits[1], and how can we understand those passages in Plautus and Cicero which clearly refer to *praedes* and *praedia* in private transactions[2]? If then we deny to *praediatura* an exclusively public character, we must class it with *sponsio* and *uadimonium* as another formal mode of giving security.

The etymology which explains the word *praes* as being the adverbial form of *praesto* is undoubtedly false[3]. Ihering and Göppert[4] suppose that it comes from the same root as *praedium,* and means one who undertakes a liability. But in the *Lex agraria* the spelling is *praeuides* instead of *praedes,* and this indicates rather that the true derivation is from *prae* and *uas*[5], in the sense of "one who comes forth and binds himself verbally"[6]. Pott[7] thinks that *uas* was the generic term for surety, and that *praes* was a composite word meaning a surety who makes good. (*praestare*) what he undertakes. Where the derivation is so uncertain no safe conclusion can be arrived at, and the origin of the contract must, in this case as in that of the primitive *uadimonium,* remain an enigma.

1 Cf. *aduersarius,* Gai. IV. 16, 94.
2 Plaut. *Men.* 4. 2. 28 ; Cic. *Att.* XIII. 3. 1.
3 Rivier, *Untersuch.* p. 29.   4 *Z. für RG.* IV. p. 263.
5 *Fas* from *fari,* or *uas* from a root meaning " to bind."
6 Dernburg, *Pfdr.* I. 27 ; Rivier, *Untersuch.* p. 14.
7 *Etym. Forsch.* IV. p. 417.

The obligation of the *praes* was enforced by compulsory sale, the details of which we unfortunately do not know. The expression *praedes uendere*[1] shows approximately how the right was enforced[2], but it is uncertain whether this[3] meant to sell the property of the surety, or merely to sell the claim of the State against him[4].

Besides the personal responsibility thus assumed by the *praes*, there was another kind of security known as *praedium*[5] which the principal might be required to give. If the *praedes* furnished by him were not sufficient, *praedium* might be required as an additional safeguard[6]; but we also find that *praedes* or *praedia* might be separately given[7].

The form in which a bond of *praedia* had to be made was a written acknowledgment in the Treasury (*praediorum apud aerarium subsignatio*), and the only object capable of serving or being pledged as a *praedium* was landed property owned by a Roman citizen, and possessing all the qualities of a *res mancipi*[8]. Hence the security of *praedia* could not in many instances have been available, for the whole of *solum prouinciale* and the holdings of *ager publicus* in the possession of *occupatorii* would of course have been excluded. The amount of

[1] Cic. *Phil.* II. 31. 78; *aes Malac. cap.* 64–5.

[2] Dernburg, *Pfdr.* I. p. 28. [3] Cic. 2 *Verr.* I. 54. 142.

[4] Göppert, *Z. für RG.* IV. p. 288.

[5] *Lex agraria* of A.V.C. 643; *Lex Put. parieti faciendo*, Bruns, *Font.* p. 272, *aes Malac. cap.* 64.

[6] *aes Malac. cap.* 60.

[7] e.g. *Lex Acilia repet.* 61, 66, 67, and Festus s.u. *quadrantal.*

[8] Cic. *Flacc.* 32. 80.

praedia which had to be given was entirely in the magistrate's discretion[1], and to help him in his decision we find that there existed *praediorum cognitores*[2] who were probably persons appointed to assess the value of *praedia*, and responsible to the State if their information was wrong.

As to the nature of the transaction effected by *praediorum subsignatio*, there can be no doubt that the old theory held by Savigny and others is incorrect[3], and that the State did not in virtue of *subsignatio* become absolute owner of the *praedia*. Rivier and Dernburg[4] have demonstrated that the State merely acquired a lien, and that *praediorum subsignatio* was therefore a species of mortgage. The classical sources fully support this view[5], and it is certain that while the property was subject to this lien its owner still had the right to sell it and to exercise other rights of ownership[6]. A public sale (*uenditio praediorum*) followed closely no doubt upon the default of the debtor, but did not necessarily accompany the sale of the goods of the *praedes*[7] (*uenditio praedium*). At Rome the former sale was made by the *praefecti aerario*, and in the *Lex Malacitana* the duumvirs or *decuriones* are empowered to make it[8].

A peculiarity of the sale of *praedia* was that the

---

[1] *Lex agraria*, 73–4 ; Bruns, *Font.* p. 84.

[2] *aes Malac. cap.* 65.

[3] Savigny *Heid. Jahrsch.* 1809, p. 268 ; Walter, *R. G.* p. 587 ; Hugo, *R. G.* 449.

[4] *Pfdr.* I. p. 33.   [5] Varro *L. L.* v. 40 ; *Lex agraria*, 74.

[6] 50 *Dig.* 17. 205.   [7] Gai. II. 61 ; Cic. 2 *Verr.* I. 55. 144.

[8] *cap.* 64; Bruns, *Font.* p. 146.

dominium residing in the owner became instantly transferred to the *praediator* or purchaser from the State, without any act on the owner's part. The only advantage reserved to the dispossessed owner was an exceptional right of recovering his property from the purchaser by *usureceptio*, i.e. conscious *usucapio*[1], one of the few instances in which it was possible to exercise *usucapio* otherwise than with a *bona fide* colour of title. In this case, as the *praedia* were always land, the statutory period of two years was necessary to complete the adverse possession.

The *lex praediatoria* mentioned in the *aes Malacitanum*[2] has been thought to be a statute of unknown date; but it more probably denotes some collection of traditional terms used in *praediatura* and analogous to a *lex uenditionis* in a contract of sale[3]. The restoration of "*praediatoria*" in Gaius[4] is doubtful, and "*censoria*" seems much to be preferred.

The operation of *praediatura* as a general lien on all the property of the *praes* was probably recognised in the Republican period, although Dernburg[5] has doubts on this point. Such a lien is found in the *Lex Malacitana* in the time of Domitian, but this may have been an extension to the public *aerarium* of the general *hypotheca* belonging to the Imperial *Fiscus*. At any rate, there is no evidence that the lien did not exist in our period; and if it

[1] Gai. II. 61. [2] *cap.* 64.
[3] Boecking, *Röm. Priv. R.* 294.
[4] IV. 28. [5] *Pfdr.* I. p. 42.

did, we can readily see that the security of *praedia-tura* was superior to that of *sponsio*.

It is perhaps natural that the subject of *praedes* and *praedia* should be obscure, for the complicated nature of the law of *praediatura* is attested by Cicero [1], who states that certain lawyers made it a special study.

Art. 4. ACTIONES ADIECTICIAE. Besides introducing the *actio mandati*, the Praetor's edict enlarged the scope of agency by instituting several other important actions. These were the *actiones quod iussu, exercitoria, institoria, tributoria, de peculio* and *de in rem uerso*. In all of them alike the Praetor's object was to fasten responsibility on some superior with whose consent, or on whose behalf, contracts had been made by an inferior. They are known as *actiones adiecticiae*, because they were considered as supplementing the ordinary actions which could be brought against the inferior himself [2]. As they made the principal liable on the contracts of a subordinate, it is plain that they must have been a most useful substitute for the complete law of agency which the Romans always lacked. The fact that they all had *formulae in ius conceptae* points to a late origin, but they all doubtless originated before the end of the Republic.

(1) The *actio quod iussu* was an action in which a son or slave, who had made a contract at the bidding of his *pater familias,* was treated as a mere conduit pipe, and by which the obligation was directly imposed on the *pater familias* who had

---

[1] *Balb.* 20. 45.　　　　[2] 14 *Dig.* 1. 5. fr. 1.

authorized it. Since Labeo mentioned the action as
though its practice was well developed in his day[1],
we may fairly suppose that *iussus* was made actionable in Republican times.

The formula was as follows:

*Quod iussu N[i] Negidii A[s] Agerius Gaio, cum is
in potestate N[i] Negidii esset, togam uendidit qua de
re agitur, quidquid ob eam rem Gaium filium A[o]
Agerio dare facere oportet ex fide bona, eius iudex
N[m] Negidium patrem A[o] Agerio condemna. s. n. p. a.*
Here the express command of the superior was the
source of his obligation.

(2) The *actio exercitoria* was an action in which
a ship owner or charterer (*exercitor*) was held directly
responsible for the contracts of the ship master[2] (*magister nauis*). Its formula probably ran as follows:
*Quod A[s] Agerius de Lucio Titio magistro eius nauis
quam N[s] Negidius exercebat, eius rei causa in quam
L[s] Titius ibi praepositus fuit, incertum stipulatus est
qua de re agitur, quidquid ob eam rem N[m] Negidium
A[o] Agerio praestare oportet ex fide bona eius N[m]
Negidium A[o] Agerio condemna. s. n. p. a.*[3] It was
known to Ofilius in the eighth century of the city[4],
and was very probably even older than his day.

The necessities of trade were obviously the source
from which this particular form of agency sprang,
because in an age of great commercial activity,
when even bills of lading were not yet introduced,
it was expedient that the delivery of goods or the

[1] 15 *Dig.* 4. 1. fr. 9.   [2] 14 *Dig.* 1. 1.
[3] Baron, *Abh. aus dem R. C. P.* II. 181.
[4] 14 *Dig.* 1. 1. fr. 9.

making of contracts by the master should be equivalent to a direct transaction with the ship owner himself.

(3) The *actio institoria* no doubt had a like commercial origin. This was an action by which the person who employed a manager (*institor*) in a business from which he drew the profits, was made liable for the debts and contracts of the manager. This action was known as early as the days of Seruius Sulpicius[1], and its formula closely resembled that of the *actio exercitoria*. The difference between these two and the *actio quod iussu* consisted simply in the fact that the *iussus* or authorization was special in the one case, and general in the other two. In the *actiones exercitoria* and *institoria* an implied general authority was ascribed to the agent in virtue of his *praepositio*[2], whereas in the *actio quod iussu* the agent had only an express special authority. Thus the *magister nauis* and the *institor* were genuine instances of general agents; and we find therefore, as we should have expected, that the acts of the *magister* and *institor* only bound the master when strictly within the scope of their authority[3]. This is an excellent instance of the manner in which Mercantile Law has developed the same rules in ancient as in modern times.

(4) The *actio tributoria* was that by which a master was compelled to pay over[4] to the creditors of a son or slave trading with his consent whatever

[1] 14 *Dig.* 3. 5. fr. 1.
[2] 46 *Dig.* 3. 18 ; Costa, *Azioni ex.* p. 40.
[3] 14 *Dig.* 1. 1. fr. 7.   [4] *tribui*, 14 *Dig.* 4. 5. 5.

profits he had received from the business. The formula ran thus: *Quod A[s] Agerius de L[o] Titio qui in potestate N[i] Negidii est, cum is sciente N[o] Negidio merce peculiari negotiaretur, incertum stipulatus est qua de re agitur, quidquid ex ea merce et quod eo nomine receptum est ob eam rem N[m] Negidium A[o] Agerio tribuere oportet, eius dumtaxat in id quod minus*[1] *dolo malo N[i] Negidii A[s] Agerius tribuit, N[m] Negidium A[o] Agerio condemna. s. n. p. a*[2]. This action was mentioned by Labeo[3] and was therefore probably as old as the other actions of this class. The knowledge and tacit approval of the superior were here the source of his obligation.

(5) The *actiones de peculio* and *de in rem uerso* were proceedings by which the master was required to make good any obligation contracted by his son or slave, to the extent of the son's or slave's *peculium*, or of such gain as had accrued to himself (*in rem uersum*) from the contract. Their peculiarity, as Gaius has told us and as a recent writer conclusively shows[4], was that they had one formula with an alternative *condemnatio*, which may be reconstructed as follows: *Quod A[s] Agerius de Lucio Titio cum is in potestate N[i] Negidii esset, incertum stipulatus est qua de re agitur, quidquid ob eam rem Lucius Titius A[o] Agerio praestare oportet ex fide bona, eius iudex N[m] Negidium A[o] Agerio, dumtaxat de peculio quod penes N[m] Negidium est, uel siquid in rem N[i] Negidii inde versum est, condemna. s. n. p. a.* This

[1] 14 *Dig.* 7. 3.   [2] Baron, *l. c.* p. 176.

[3] 14 *Dig.* 4. 7.

[4] Baron, *l. c.* pp. 136–69 ; cf. Lenel, *Ed. perp.* p. 225.

formula might be so modified that the *actio de peculio* and the *actio de in rem uerso* could be brought either separately or together. These actions were known to Alfenus Varus[1], and it is safe to say that they were introduced some time before the end of the Republic. The knowledge or consent of the superior did not here have to be proved.

The difference between the *actio tributoria* and the *actio de peculio* was considerable. By the former the master contributed his profits and then shared in the distribution as an ordinary creditor. But by the latter he became a preferred creditor, and deducted from his profits the whole amount owed to him by the son or slave. The *peculium* in the latter case was in fact only the balance remaining after the debts of the son to him had been satisfied.

Art. 5. CONSTITVTVM AND RECEPTVM. Towards the end of the Republic we find two kinds of formless contract by which a debt could be created, and both of which seem to have sprung from the requirements of Roman commerce[2].

I. Constitutum.

The chief characteristics of this contract may be gathered from the constitution by which Justinian fused together the *actio recepticia* and the *actio pecuniae constitutae*[3], as well as from allusions in the Digest. It seems to have been a formless promise of payment at a particular date; depending on the existence of a prior indebtedness to which the

[1] 15 *Dig.* 3. 16.   [2] Ihering, *Geist* iv. 218–220.

[3] 4 *Cod.* 18. 2.

constitutum became accessory[1]; unconditional[2]; enforced by an *actio pecuniae constitutae* of Praetorian origin which was in some cases *perpetua* and in others *annalis*; and available to persons of all classes.

Constitutum is discussed by Labeo[3], and is mentioned by Cicero[4] in a way which makes it certain that the *actio pecuniae constitutae* existed in his day. The action originated in the Praetor's Edict[5], and it was thereby provided with a penal *sponsio* similar to that of the *condictio certae pecuniae*. This leads us to infer that *pecunia constituta* was treated by the Praetor as analogous to *pecunia credita*; especially as Gaius[6] states that *pecunia credita* strictly meant only an unconditional obligation to pay money, while we know from Justinian's constitution that unless *constitutum* was unconditional no action would lie. But why should the penal *sponsio* of the *actio pecuniae constitutae* have been so much heavier than that of the *condictio*, namely *dimidiae* instead of *tertiae partis*[7]? The reason given by Theophilus[8] is that *constitutum* was generally entered into by a debtor in order to gain time for the payment of a debt *already* due, and that the Praetor instituted this severe action in order to discourage insolvent debtors from this practice. Labeo on the contrary says[9] that *constitutum* was made actionable in order to enforce the payment of debts *not* yet due. Both

[1] 13 *Dig.* 5. 1. fr. 5
[2] *Cod. l. c.*
[3] 13 *Dig.* 5. 3.
[4] *Quint.* 5. 18.
[5] 13 *Dig.* 5. 16.
[6] III. 124.
[7] Gai. IV. 171.
[8] *Paraphr.* IV. 6–8.
[9] 13 *Dig.* 5. 3.

Labeo and Theophilus are probably right[1], but each takes a one-sided view. The Praetor's aim presumably was to enforce the payment of any debt, due or not due, which the debtor had made a renewed promise to pay at a particular date. The breach of a repeated promise (for *constitutum* always implied a previous promise or indebtedness) was doubtless regarded by the Praetor as a singularly flagrant breach of faith ; and hence he compelled the defendant to join in a penal *sponsio dimidiae partis*.

This *actio per sponsionem* was not however the only remedy for a breach of *constitutum*. The Digest shows that the usual form of redress was an *actio in factum*[2], which[3] probably had a formula as follows : *Si paret Numerium Negidium Aulo Agerio X millia Kal. Ian. se soluturum constituisse, neque eam pecuniam soluisse, neque per Agerium stetisse quominus solueretur, eamque pecuniam cum constituebatur debitam fuisse, quanti ea res est, tantam pecuniam Numerium Negidium Aulo Agerio condemna* ; and that this *actio in factum* existed in Gaius' time as an alternative remedy seems probable from his language in IV. 171. It is not likely that the *actio in factum* arose simultaneously with the other ; and of the two Puchta[4] is almost certainly right in assigning the earlier date to the *actio per sponsionem*, because the custom of *sponsione prouocare* suggests an ancient origin. This *sponsio*, like that of the *condictio*, was *praeiudicialis*, but it also contained a strongly penal element. Its penal character was

[1] Bruns, *Z. f. RG.* I. p. 56.　　[2] 13 *Dig.* 5. 16. 2.

[3] Bruns, *loc. cit.* p. 59.　　[4] *Inst.* II. 168.

no doubt the reason why the action could not be brought against the heir of the *constituens*, and why it was *annalis*. As Bruns has shown, the remedy after one year was probably the *actio in factum*[1], by which the plain amount of the *constitutum* could alone be recovered.

Constitutum could be employed for the renewal of the promisor's own debt (*const. debiti proprii*), as well as of another man's (*const. debiti alieni*), and this distinction was early allowed[2]. In the later law it could also be used to reinforce and render actionable an *obligatio naturalis*. But this feature probably did not exist at the origin of the action[3], for the Praetor could only have had in mind *pecunia credita*, when he inflicted such a heavy penalty. The effect of *constitutum* was simply to reinforce the old obligation by supplying a more stringent remedy. It never produced novation as *stipulatio* or *expensilatio*[4] would have done.

II. Receptum.

The agreement by which shipmasters, innkeepers and stablemen (*nautae, caupones, stabularii*) undertook to take care of the goods or property of their customers was known as *receptum*, and was enforced by means of an *actio de recepto* as rigorously as the duties of common carriers are enforced by the Common Law[5]. The Edict was expressed as follows: NAVTAE CAVPONES STABVLARII QVOD CVIVSQVE SALVVM FORE RECEPERINT NISI RESTITVENT, IN EOS IVDICIVM DABO ;

---

[1] Bruns, *loc. cit.* p. 68.   [2] 13 *Dig.* 5. 2.

[3] Bruns, *ib.* p. 69.   [4] 13 *Dig.* 5. 28.

[5] Carnazza, *Dir. Com.* p. 106.

and the remedy was an ordinary *actio in factum*, authorising the judge to assess damages for the loss or non-production of the goods.

But the contract which more nearly concerns us is *receptum argentariorum*, the nature of which has been a subject of much controversy.

This was a formless promise to pay on behalf of another man, and we gather from Justinian[1] that it was capable of creating an original debt; capable of being made *sub conditione* or *in diem*, and enforced by an *actio recepticia*, which was *perpetua;* while Theophilus tells us[2] that it was confined to bankers (*argentarii*). Bruns[3] indeed supposes that *receptum* was a formal contract *iuris ciuilis*, while according to Voigt[4] it was a species of *expensilatio* devised by the *argentarii*. Lenel[5] however has proved that *receptum argentariorum* was introduced and regulated by the Praetor in the same part of the Edict in which he treated of the *recepta nautarum, cauponarum* and *stabulariorum*. This appears from the fact that in 13 *Dig.* 5. 27 and 28, *constituere* has evidently been substituted by Tribonian and his colleagues for *recipere*. Ulpian treated of *constitutum* in his 27th book on the Edict[6]: but the passage quoted in the Digest is from his 14th book on the Edict, in which we know[7] that he discussed the clause *Nautae caupones stabularii*. So also Pomponius, who discussed *recepta*

[1] 4 *Cod.* 18. 2.   [2] IV. 6–8.   [3] *Z. für RG.* I. 51 ff.

[4] *Röm. RG.* I. 65–8.   [5] *Z. der Sav. Stift.* II. 62 ff.

[6] 13 *Dig.* 5. 16.   [7] 4 *Dig.* 9. 1.

nautarum &c. in his 34th book[1] and *constitutum* in his 8th[2], is described[3] as mentioning the latter in his 34th book. Gaius also is represented to have dealt with *constitutum* in the very same book[4] in which he treated of *recepta nautarum*[5].

We must conclude, either that all these writers introduced into their discussion of *recepta nautarum* &c. the totally irrelevant subject of *constitutum*, or that the subject thus introduced was not *constitutum* but *receptum argentariorum*. If the latter conclusion is correct, as we may well believe that it must be, it follows that *receptum argentariorum* was, like the other *recepta*, regulated by the Praetorian Edict, and was therefore not a contract *iuris ciuilis*. By analogy with the other *recepta* we may further conclude that *receptum argentariorum* was formless, and hence cannot have been a species of *expensilatio*. The remedy was of course an *actio in factum*.

Recipere is used by Cicero[6] in the sense of undertaking a personal guarantee, but with no clearly technical meaning. Justinian states that the *actio recepticia* was objectionable on account of its "*solemnia uerba*," and Lenel has explained this to mean that the *actio recepticia*, being necessarily *in factum* like those of the other *recepta*, had to contain the words "*si paret......soluturum recepisse......neque soluisse quod solui recepit*," of which *recipere* was a technical term. This term, being misunderstood by the Greeks, was translated in Justinian's time

---

[1] 4 *Dig.* 9. 1 fr. 7 and 9. 3. [2] 13 *Dig.* 5. 5 fr. 5.
[3] *ib.* 5. 27.   [4] *ib.* 5. 28.   [5] 4 *Dig.* 9. 2 and 5.
[6] *Phil.* v. 18. 51.; *ad Fam.* XIII. 17.

by *constituere*. It is almost certain that the *actio recepticia* was known before the end of the Republic, since Labeo evidently [1] discussed it.

The function of *receptum* probably was to provide an international mode of assigning indebtedness, because *transcriptio a persona in personam* was not available to peregrins [2]. The existence of the debt between the creditor and the original debtor was clearly not affected by the obligation of the *argentarius* who had made a *receptum*; and from the passages above cited Lenel also infers that *receptum pro alio* was the only known form which the contract ever took. In short, it seems to have closely resembled the acceptance of a modern bill of exchange [3], and it was doubtless made by the *argentarius* on behalf of his clients or correspondents.

[1] 13 *Dig.* 5. 27.   [2] Lenel, *Z. der Sav. Stift.* II. 70.
[3] Carnazza, *Dir. Com.* p. 93.

CONCLUSION.

We have now traced the development of the Roman Law of Contract from an early stage of Formalism, in which few agreements were actionable, and those few provided with imperfect remedies, to the almost complete maturity to which it had attained by the end of the Republic.

Of all the contracts which we have examined, *nexum* and *uadimonium* seem to be the only two that became obsolete during this period, while the new contracts of Praetorian origin, such as *depositum* and *constitutum*, attained their full growth, as we have seen; so that the jurists of the Empire found little to do besides the work of interpretation and amplification.

The one great improvement, and almost the only one, which the Law of Contract underwent subsequently to our period, was the introduction of the *actiones praescriptis uerbis,* by which the scope of Real Contract was immensely enlarged.

In other respects, the Law of the Republic has the credit of having generated that wonderful system of Contract which later ages have scarcely ever failed to copy, and which lies at the root of so much of English Law.

INDEX.

Printed by Printforce, United Kingdom